Handbook
to the
Deschutes River Canyon

By:
James M. Quinn
James W. Quinn
James G. King

Frank Amato Publications
Portland, Oregon

To my teams which have given their community a record of excellence and a source of pride.

An introduction to **EDUCATIONAL ADVENTURES, INCORPORATED:**

This unique concept coordinates adventure *and* education. As you travel down each river, we believe your journeys will take on additional meaning if you become more familiar with your environment. Each handbook is designed to share the knowledge of professional guides who make their livelihoods from the rivers. We touch upon the humor, pathos, tragedy and personal experiences of people who lived, worked and contributed to the history of the rivers. A little physical and biological science is included to clarify the delicate ecological balances which are in effect and which link the present to both the past and the future. It is our wish that, at the end of each river journey, you will feel that your adventure has added to the richness of your life. Thank you for purchasing our handbooks. The profits realized from their sales will give us the means to write handbooks on as many rivers as we can . . .

Additional copies of the Guide Handbooks may be ordered from:

Frank Amato Publications
P.O. Box 82112
Portland, Oregon 97282
(503) 653-8108

Other book available
Handbook to the Rogue River Canyon
Handbook to the Middle Fork of the Salmon River
Handbook to the Illinois River Canyon
Handbook to the Klamath River Canyon
Hell's Corner Gorge of the Upper Klamath
    (waterproof map)
Hells Canyon of the Snake River
    (waterproof map)

THIRD EDITION

Library of Congress Cataloging in Publication Data

Library of Congress Catalog Card Number: 79-64360

ISBN: 1-878175-35-1
Printed in Hong Kong

CONTENTS

Note to New Printing:

Since this book was originally written, several important changes have occured on the Deschutes River that you should know. If you are floating any part of the lower river from Warms Springs Bridge to the mouth (approximately 97 miles) it is necessary to have a Deschutes River Boaters Pass for each person in your party. These are available from the Oregon Department of Parks in Salem, as well as many sporting goods stores in Portland and general stores in towns close to the river such as The Dalles, Maupin and Madras. Cost is $1.75 per day, or $12.00 for the year. Read carefully the booklet that comes with your pass for up-to-date regulations concerning fire seasons and required stove and lantern types and camping. This fee is reinvested in the river's management.

If you plan to fish, obtain a copy of the angling regulations wherever fishing licenses are sold. Because of angler-led requests by the Northwest Steelheaders, Angler's Club of Portland, Oregon Trout (and others), the lower 97 miles of the river are now managed to protect wild, resident trout and migratory summer steelhead, including the rare Dolly Varden. For that reason very good trout fishing with barbless hook flies and lures is available, especially from Warm Springs to below Maupin.

Naturally, you must carry out your own litter. But please carry out in your boat any other refuse you see. Its simple to do and leaves a nice river experience for all of us. Have a great trip!

IMPORTANT WARNING!

Virtually all major rapids change dramatically with minor fluctuations in streamflow. "How To" instructions in this book are applicable to intermediate water levels only. Extremes of high and low water volumes must be considered as completely different situations, and must be scouted for oneself. The Deschutes River will often double in flow volume, ranging from 3,000 to 10,000 cfs.

Of course, unexpected situations will occur. Rocks, slides, earthquakes, floods, winds and other natural and man-made phenomena can change any piece of whitewater or stillwater overnight. You must remain alert at all times and use common-sense as you travel down this (or any) river. Good judgment is your best ally.

As a rule, if you cannot see from the beginning to the end of a piece of whitewater, don't enter it. Get out and scout before committing your vessel and yourself to its powerful forces. Even if you can see the entry and exit of the rapids, don't enter it if there is any suspicion that submerged boulders, ledges or protruding obstructions exist. Get out and scout it.

There is no book written which can teach you as much as your own experience, and no amount of words can save your life or prevent your injuries. Take care of yourself, think ahead, use good boatmanship and self-preservation logic. Remain skeptical. Use caution. Think . . .

ACKNOWLEDGEMENTS

Perhaps the most enjoyable part of writing this book was meeting the people that have contributed to the history of the Deschutes Canyon. We owe many thanks to Mrs. H. E. Carleton of Dufur for sharing the memories of her husband's railroad construction days.

Special appreciation and gratitude are extended to J. C. Meyers and Ted Lewis for supplying an endless source of Oregon Trunk Railroad history. Both men have spent their entire lives serving the Railroad.

A sincere thanks to Don Turcke for his special interest in the students at Waldport High School.

We would also like to thank Mrs. Avis Fowler for her early day memories of the Railroad Construction Era.

Great appreciation is expressed to Jim Pond for his excellent cartography used in this book.

Several professional guides have examined the river log and offered helpful comments and advice. We would like to express our sincere appreciation to Oscar Lange for sharing his 30 years of guiding experience with us. Also, thanks to river guide Mike McLucas. We are also indebted to Waldport High School librarian Sue Lake, for her help in collecting research material.

We would like to thank Mark Angel for sharing his knowledge and experience.

Many thanks to the Bend Bulletin and the staff of the Deschutes County Historical Society for their help.

UPPER DESCHUTES ACCESS MAP

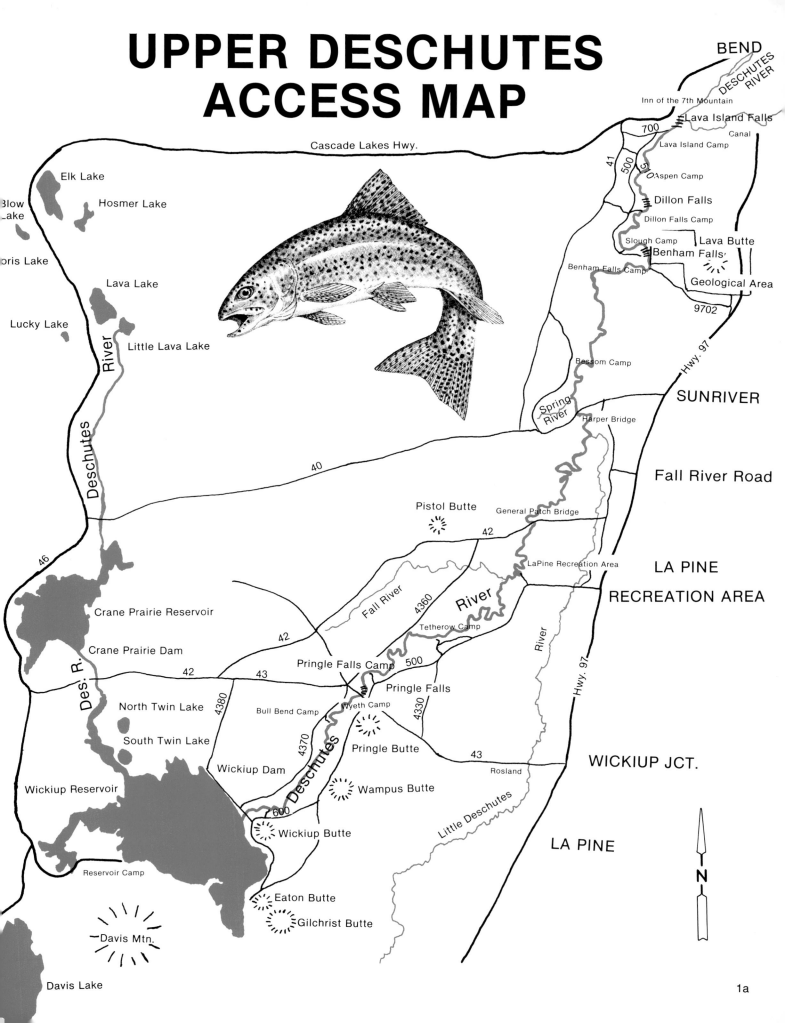

BEND

DESCHUTES RIVER

Cascade Lakes Hwy.

Elk Lake

Blow Lake

Hosmer Lake

oris Lake

Lava Lake

Lucky Lake

Little Lava Lake

River

Deschutes

Inn of the 7th Mountain

Lava Island Falls

Canal

700

Lava Island Camp

41

500

510

Aspen Camp

Dillon Falls

Dillon Falls Camp

Slough Camp

Lava Butte

Benham Falls

Benham Falls Camp

Geological Area

9702

Bessom Camp

Hwy. 97

SUNRIVER

Spring River

Harper Bridge

40

Fall River Road

Pistol Butte

General Patch Bridge

42

LaPine Recreation Area

LA PINE

RECREATION AREA

46

Crane Prairie Reservoir

Fall River

4360

River

Tetherow Camp

Crane Prairie Dam

42

Pringle Falls Camp

500

Des. R.

42

43

North Twin Lake

4380

Bull Bend Camp

Wyeth Camp

Pringle Falls

4330

River

Hwy. 97

South Twin Lake

4370

Deschutes

Pringle Butte

43

Rosland

WICKIUP JCT.

Wickiup Dam

Wampus Butte

Wickiup Reservoir

600

Little Deschutes

LA PINE

Wickiup Butte

Reservoir Camp

N

Eaton Butte

Gilchrist Butte

Davis Mtn.

Davis Lake

1a

UPPER DESCHUTES

The Deschutes River gains its sustenance from the snow-covered peaks of the Cascades.

The river springs to life along the southwestern shore of Little Lava Lake. A U.S. Geological Survey report states: "The flow of the Deschutes is more constant and uniform than any other river in the United States of comparable volume." This can be attributed to the numerous springs that nourish the river. These tributaries are supplied by underground lava tubes that carry snow melt from the slopes of snow-covered mountains many miles away.

The Deschutes drains a watershed larger than the state of Maryland. From its mile-high beginnings the river cuts a path through forests and lava as it flows 252 miles to join the Columbia.

The river's journey is detoured at Crane Prairie Reservoir, the first of several man-made lakes to impede the river's progress. The former river channel is marked on both sides by a dead lodgepole pine forest extending out of the slack waters. The bleached tree skeletons afford shelter to the huge fish, and nesting sites for the many birds of prey. The large trout and numerous osprey that inhabit

Osprey at Crane Prairie Reservoir.
Courtesy Oregon Department of Fish and Game

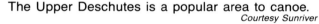

The Upper Deschutes is a popular area to canoe.
Courtesy Sunriver

the reservoir have made Crane Prairie famous.

A short distance below Crane Prairie the Deschutes is blocked a second time, forming Wickiup Reservoir. The waters behind this dam produce some of the finest trout fishing in Oregon. Below Wickiup the Deschutes flows north.

The liberated river begins in a slow and meandering manner. From Wickiup to Bend the average stream flow is less than two miles per hour. The placid waters are only interrupted once for a distance of forty miles. At Pringle Falls, rocks and strong hydraulics render the Deschutes unsafe to float.

At Benham Falls the river follows the west side of a large lava flow. The resistant basalt has held its own against the river, creating many rapids and several waterfalls. At Lava Island the hydraulics increase. The river resembles a millrace punctuated with dangerous rapids and impassible falls.

A short distance above Bend much of the Deschutes is drained off for irrigation. During the growing season, the water is diverted into 210 miles of main canals and 718 miles of ditches. From April until October, the Deschutes is too low to float from Bend to Lake Billy Chinook.

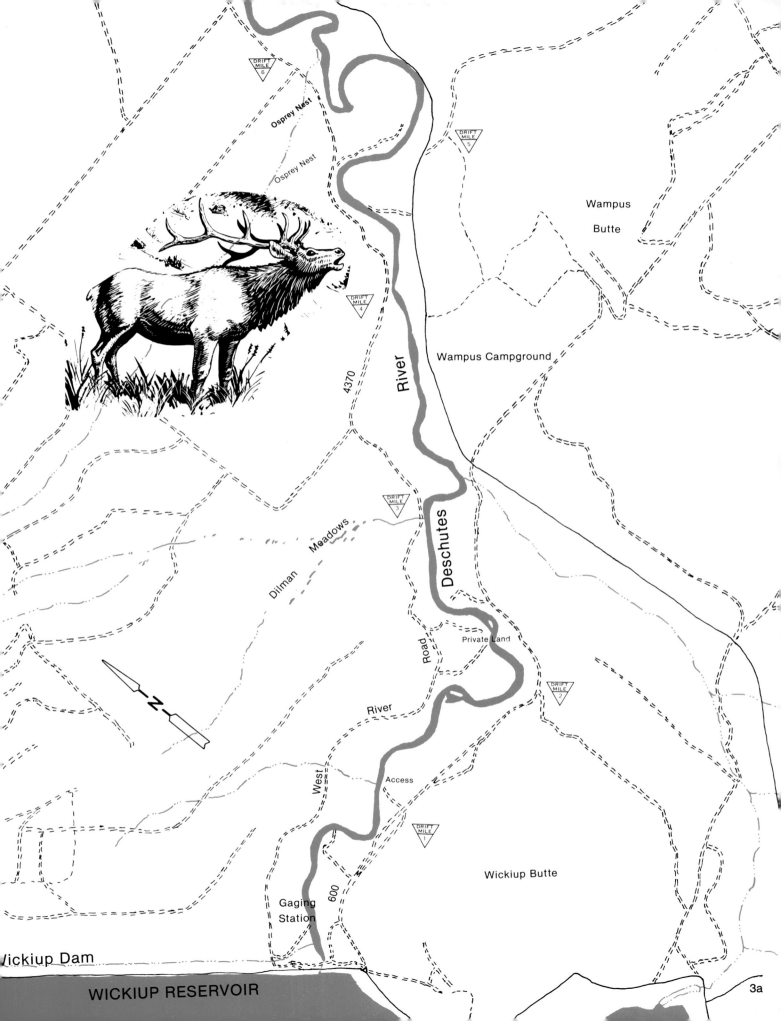

DRIFT
MILE
6

Osprey Nest

Osprey Nest

Wampus

Butte

DRIFT
MILE
5

DRIFT
MILE
4

4370

River

Wampus Campground

Deschutes

DRIFT
MILE
3

Meadows

Dilman

Private Land

Road

DRIFT
MILE
2

N

River

Access

West

DRIFT
MILE
1

Wickiup Butte

600

Gaging
Station

Wickiup Dam

WICKIUP RESERVOIR

3a

The river from Wickiup Dam to Wyeth Campground is Class I. The river length is 8.4 miles and the shuttle distance is 9.2 miles. To reach the put-in, take the road past the dam-keeper's house on the east end of Wickiup Dam. Proceed N.E. 3 miles, turn left and drive to the river. To reach the take-out, cross over to the west end of Wickiup Dam, turn right, N.E. on Rd. 4370 to Wyeth Campground. You must take out here. There is no landing between Wyeth Camp and Pringle Falls. **DO NOT attempt Pringle Falls. It is extremely dangerous.** There is an intermediate put-in and take out at Bull Bend Campground.

Wickiup Reservoir

0.0

When Indians moved to a new home, they threw up quick, temporary shelters made out of branches and boughs and sapling poles. Those shelters were called wickiups. In the fall, the Indians would gather at a point a few miles south of Crane Prairie to hunt and fish. When they left, they left the poles of their crude structures behind, and the area came to be called Wickiups. When a dam was built on what is now the eastern edge of the reservoir, the dam and reservoir naturally took the same name.

The Deschutes between Bend and Wickiup Reservoir doesn't have the prolific brown trout fishery it did before siltation covered many spawning beds. The fame of Wickiup and Crane Prairie reservoirs, with their trout approaching 20 pounds, has overshadowed the river downstream from Wickiup. But it's still possible to pick up big browns in the river.

The Deschutes River and its source, Little Lava Lake, have been the stages for at least three unsolved murder cases, including one which happened more than 50 years ago.

In 1924, three trappers were found murdered in Little Lava Lake, where the Deschutes begins its 252-mile journey. It was on April 13, 1924, that the Little Lava Lake mystery began to unfold. Dewey Morris, 24, Ed Nichols, 50, and Roy Wilson, 36, seasoned trappers, were overdue in Bend from their camp at a fox farm near the lake after a winter's work. Relatives had expected them to return from the forest in late February. After nearly two months passed and they still hadn't returned, Morris' brother, Owen, set out with another man for the camp. They were alarmed by what they found. The trappers were nowhere to be seen. But their dirty breakfast dishes sat on the dining table, and a pot of food lay mildewing on the stove. Their hats, coats, traps and guns remained in the cabin.

Deschutes County sheriff's deputies were called in. In the next few days, they found telling bits of evidence, a sled marked with what appeared to be blood stains, tracks leading to the lake's edge, and, 150 feet out from shore in line with the sled tracks, a hole cut in the ice. The deputies probed the chilly depths beneath the hole, but to no avail. Then on April 23, 10 days after the men were found to be missing, the spring warmth began to break up the ice. And there, bobbing on the surface near where the ice hole had been, three bodies were discovered. After recovering the corpses, the deputies discovered each man had been shot in the back of the head.

The only lead was the fact that a man matching the description of one Charles Kimzey, alias Lee Collins, on April 21 was reported to have sold the stolen fox furs to dealers in Klamath Falls and Portland. Kimzey was an escaped convict from Idaho. He also was wanted for the attempted murder of a taxi driver, who had been poisoned, knocked out and thrown head first into a dry well in the Oregon desert.

Kimsey eluded authorities for nine years, until, at age 47, he made the mistake of showing his face in Kalispell, Mon., where he was apprehended on Feb. 16, 1933. He was brought back to Oregon and convicted not for the murders, but for the asault on the cabbie. Not enough evidence was found to link him to the killings, the motive of which some guessed lay in revenge. In 1923, the trappers apparently had supplied police with information that nearly resulted in Kimzey's capture in Idaho. Kimzey was sentenced to life in Oregon State Penitentiary. he was paroled in 1957 and is now presumed dead.

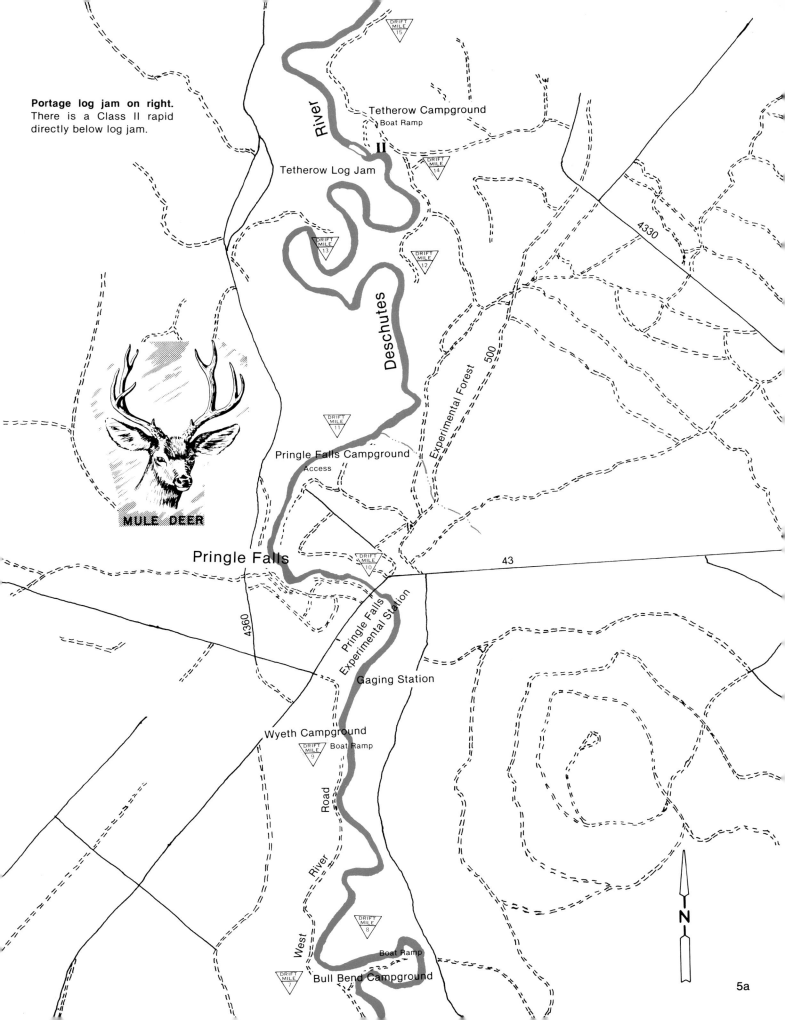

Portage log jam on right.
There is a Class II rapid directly below log jam.

River

Deschutes

DRIFT MILE 15

Tetherow Campground
Boat Ramp

II

Tetherow Log Jam

DRIFT MILE 14

DRIFT MILE 13

DRIFT MILE 12

4330

Experimental Forest 500

DRIFT MILE 11

Pringle Falls Campground

Access

MULE DEER

Pringle Falls

DRIFT MILE 10

43

4360

Pringle Falls Experimental Station

Gaging Station

Wyeth Campground

DRIFT MILE 9

Boat Ramp

Road

River

West

DRIFT MILE 8

Boat Ramp

DRIFT MILE 7

Bull Bend Campground

N

5a

9.0

Wyeth Campground is named after early day trapper and explorer **Nathaniel J. Wyeth.** On Jan. 14, 1835, Wyeth camped at this site. The following is an excerpt from his journal:

"14th Snowed about 4 inches last night. Today pretty cold. Passed the night on the south side of the south channel, there being a small island at this place. Just above the island there is a raft of drift timber which extends across the whole river. This we made a portage of for about 6 rods. At the rapid I hauled the canoe, wading in the water about waist deep and remaining in it about three hours and got quite numb, but at last got through with it.

"We then ascended the river 3 miles more in good water, but very winding, S.W. to make which I think we paddled 8 miles to another rapid not so severe. Finding that it would take some time and being obliged to return to camp soon, concluded not to pass this rapid and returned to the first rapid and set 6 traps. Day windy from the S.W. and some snow and sunshine."

9.9

Pringle Falls

On April 15, 1846, the family of Virgil K. Pringle left Missouri for the Pacific Northwest, arriving in Salem on Christmas Day the same year. The entire trip is chronicled by Pringle's son, Octavius M. Pringle, in a document called Experiences of an Emigrant Boy of 1846. It is the younger Pringle after whom the falls were named.

Octavius Pringle moved to Central Oregon from Salem in 1874 and in 1902 bought 160 acres of land from the government near the falls under the Timber and Stone Act.

A log jam forming at Pringle Falls. For details refer to the following page.
Courtesy Deschutes County Historical Society

The following is taken from the May 1939 monthly edition of Brooks-Scanlon's **Pine Echoes.** *This article refers to a picture of Shevlin-Hixon Company's last log drive.*

It may seem strange that Brooks-Scanlon should use a cover of this nature, but we like to get sensational or outstanding pictures for the Pine Echoes, and when The Shevlin-Hixon Company, our friendly competitor across the river, decided to stage a regular old-time log drive down the Deschutes River into the mills at Bend, we had to get the picture. The Shevlin people are driving 26 million feet of logs about forty miles down stream through some of the fastest water in the upper river.

Here is a log jam forming in the narrow, dangerous Pringle Falls channel and the crew of expert white water men is working desperately to get the logs through before others can come down the river and pile up on them. When this picture was taken the men were breaking the jams with peavies, the same as they used to do in Maine and Minnesota 50 years ago, but now a huge Caterpillar tractor hooks a line on a key log and walks off with the whole jam.

This is highly dangerous and exciting work, but the loggers take it casually in the day's stride. This is no doubt the last drive down the Deschutes and will probably be the last big drive in Oregon.

10.5   The river from Pringle Falls Campground to Tetherow log jam is Class I. **At the log jam, it is necessary to portage on the right bank.** The portage is short, followed by a Class II rapid. Tetherow boat ramp is immediately below on right. The river length is 3.9 miles and the shuttle distance is the same. To reach the put-in from Wyeth Camp, cross the river on Hwy. 43. Proceed N.E. on Rd. 500 on the east side of Pringle Falls. Drive .3 miles and turn left at Pringle Falls campground. To reach **take-out,** continue down Rd. 500. When Rd. 500 joins Rd. 4330, turn left, proceed .3 mile and turn left on Rd. 2027B at boat ramp sign. The take-out is on the right bank, below Tetherow log jam.

In the past fishing the Upper Deschutes has produced many fine catches.

Courtesy Deschutes County Historical Society

Bates Butte

Fall River Falls

Fall River

Foster Ranch

Access

Big Tree

Largest Ponderosa Pine In Oregon

The Dead Slough

River

Access

Deschutes

Access

Otter

N

DRIFT MILE 25
DRIFT MILE 24
DRIFT MILE 23
DRIFT MILE 22
DRIFT MILE 21
DRIFT MILE 20
DRIFT MILE 20
DRIFT MILE 19
DRIFT MILE 18
DRIFT MILE 17
DRIFT MILE 16

14.1   The river from Tetherow Campground to Besson Camp is Class I. **Most of the land is private** along this 23.6-mile section of the Deschutes. Put in at Tetherow boat ramp. To reach take-out, return to Hwy. 97. Continue north on Hwy 97 to Sunriver. Cross Harper's Bridge, and drive to Besson Rd., turn right and continue to Besson Camp sign; turn right and drive to boat ramp. Intermediate put-ins and take-outs: Big River Camp, LaPine State Park, and Harper's Bridge.

21.2   *Fall River heads into giant springs near the Fall River Guard Station, about 12 miles west of U.S. Highway 97 on the Cascade Lakes Highway. It flows through pine woods for some eight or 10 miles before joining the Deschutes River from the west. about halfway between the source of the river and its mouth, it descends in a series of small falls and cascades.*

Roughly five environmental zones exist on the length of the Deschutes. The first is made up primarily of ponderosa pine, bitterbrush and western needlegrass. This area is good summer range for mule deer, and it is more adapted to sheep grazing than cattle.

The second zone is dominated by ponderosa pine, bitterbrush, manzanita and Idaho fescue. If water is provided, this area has good potential for livestock range.

A related zone is that characterized by ponderosa, snowbrush, fescue and bitterbrush. This zone is at slightly lower elevation than the second zone, and it is only marginal for livestock grazing use.

Another common area along the Deschutes consists of lodgepole pine, bitterbrush and Idaho fescue. At elevations from 4,200 to 5,700 feet, mule deer use the area for spring and summer forage, and it is adequate for livestock if fencing and water are provided.

Portions of the river lying close to flatter, wetter areas are dominated by various sedges and rushes, with occasional strong colonies of reedgrass. "Wet meadow" zones can be quite delicate and require grazing controls to prevent soil damage.

Maybe the naturalist, Aldo Leopold, was thinking of the eagle when he said, "There are some who can live without wild things and some who cannot. Something there is about the great birds flight that gives the spirit a lift. For those of us who cannot live without this kind of inspiration the responsibility is clear. We must take the lead in efforts to protect wild things. If we don't, no one else will."

Courtesy Oregon Department of Fish and Game

Little

Deschutes

Vandevert Ranch

Vandevert

River

River

DRIFT MILE 33

Private Land

DRIFT MILE 32

Private Land

DRIFT MILE 31

Private Land

Montgomery Ranch

DRIFT MILE 30

Deschutes

DRIFT MILE 29

DRIFT MILE 28

N

DRIFT MILE 27

GREAT HORNED OWL

General Patch Bridge

Big River Campground

DRIFT MILE 26

10a

Little Deschutes

According to Lewis A. McArthur, author of Oregon Geographic Names, *the feds originally named the Little Deschutes the East Fork. At the same time, he writes, it was called the Little River by local residents.*

In 1926, McArthur decided to take matters into his own hands and remedy the discrepency. He suggested the United States Board of Geographic Names rename the East Fork the Little Deschutes River. It did, and the name has been in general use ever since.

Zig-zagging through its 71-mile course that begins in northern Klamath County, the river shares many of its big daddy's attributes, including good fishing opportunities.

In 1915, Masten sawmill at Rosland, about one mile north of LaPine, had been supplying lumber to Bend. This material was being hauled by team or trucked by solid rubber-tired vehicles.

In 1917, new management took over Masten mill. The new owners decided to try moving the lumber by water because it would be cheaper and save time to float the 25 miles to just above Benham Falls. At that point the lumber would be trucked the remaining 12 or 14 miles to Bend. (Just above Benham Falls is as close to Bend as one could transport lumber or logs by water because the river at that point presented tortuous rapids.)

Initially, lumber was floated down the river piece by piece, but the boards either sank, piled up against the banks or were lodged somewhere in the Little Deschutes stream, jamming the river for about two miles downstream.

The Lumber company then recognized that it wasn't possible to transport the lumber in that way. Men were hired to help clean up the lumber jam, and the idea evolved of making individual rafts of about 1,000 board feet of lumber. The whole mill crew assisted.

Workers broke up the jam, caught the individual pieces of lumber, put them in raft formation and bolted them together at each end with cross ties. Then they bolted each individual raft to the one just above it with a 10-foot-long 2x12, which was bolted to the cross ties of the individual rafts. The purpose of the 10-foot connecting plank was to permit snakelike action of the whole raft so they could negotiate the many twists, bends and turns of the river. They made 42 individual rafts.

Negotiating the long raft under the various bridges, such as Harper Bridge (just south of present-day Sunriver), was hazardous at best, though in nearly all cases, safely accomplished. One worker recalls: ''As the logs passed under Vandevert footbridge on the Little Deschutes, the braking pole at the tail end of the raft caught on the footbridge. Down came the bridge, along with its owner, Claude Vandevert, who was standing on it. The bridge landed on the last raft and Vandevert was dumped into the river. Fortunately, Claude escaped with only dampened spirits. This method of transporting lumber did not prove profitable and was soon abandoned.

Early day logging near Pringle Falls.
Courtesy Deschutes County Historical Society

Early day duck hunting trip near Sunriver.
Courtesy Deschutes County Historical Society

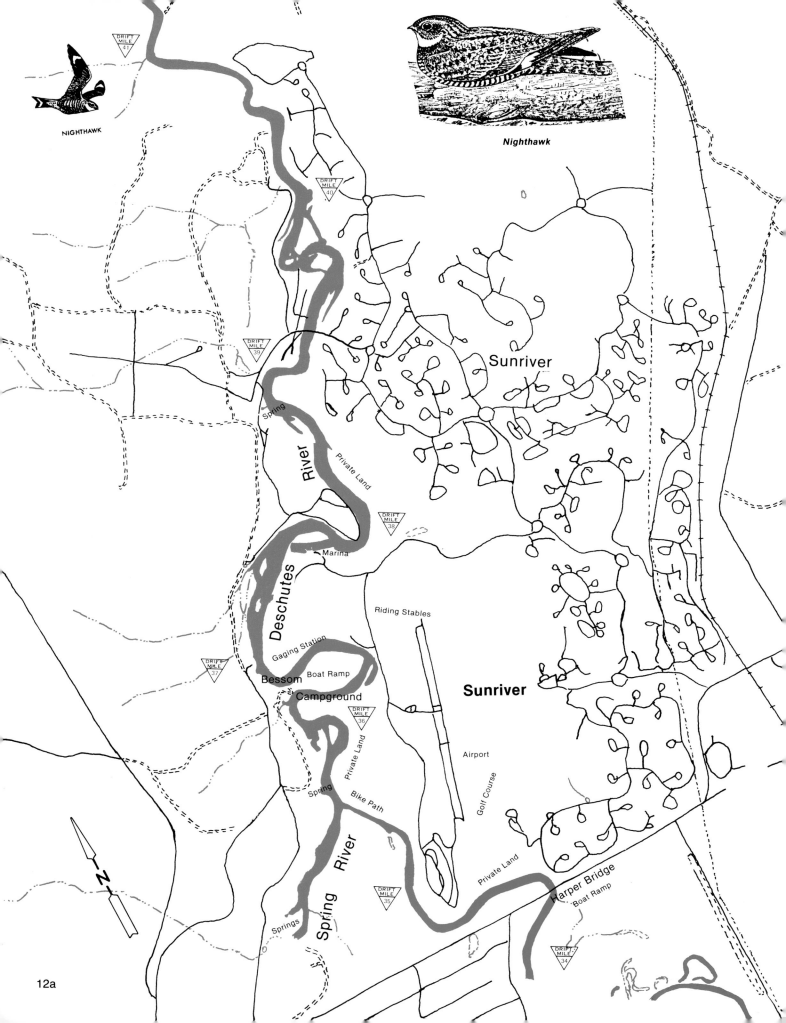

NIGHTHAWK

Nighthawk

DRIFT MILE 41

DRIFT MILE 40

DRIFT MILE 39

Sunriver

Spring

River

Private Land

DRIFT MILE 38

Marina

Deschutes

Riding Stables

Gaging Station

DRIFT MILE 37

Boat Ramp

Bessom

Campground

DRIFT MILE 36

Sunriver

Private Land

Airport

Spring

Bike Path

Golf Course

Spring River

N

Springs

DRIFT MILE 35

Private Land

Harper Bridge

Boat Ramp

DRIFT MILE 34

12a

35.0   *Sunriver* is a 3,370 acre resort and residential community. Facilities at the resort include two 18-hole golf courses, 18 tennis courts, 20 miles of paved bike paths, two swimming pool complexes, a racquetball club, stables, marina, a jogging course, nature center, arts and crafts center, game room and a bicycle and cross-country ski pavilion. Sunriver's 4,500 foot paved and lighted airstrip is the third busiest private airport in Oregon and one of the longest private airstrips in the west.

Camp Abbot

    For a year near the end of World War II, much of the area which is now Sunriver was a training center called Camp Abbot, built to accommodate 10,000 troops. In the 13 months that the camp was in operation, Bend was turned topsy-turvy. The old St. Charles Memorial Hospital in downtown Bend built a temporary wing to cope with the increased population. The base, which was dedicated Sept. 2, 1943, was named for Brig. Gen. Henry Larcom Abbot, who had camped on the spot the night of Sept. 2, 1855, with the Williamson railroad survey party he commanded.

    The Camp Abbot Officers Club, now Sunriver's Great Hall, and the flag pole which stood at the end of the main street, are all that remain of the old training camp. It is a massive hall built of hand-hewn timbers, with a bridge-like suspended balcony circling the massive open-beamed central area. A spiral staircase circles a giant ponderosa pine that was left in the spot where it grew. The Officers Club occupied its impressive new quarters in time for just one dance. The war was winding down, and Abbot was abandoned in June 1944.

    There have been many drownings on the river. One of the more tragic accidents came nearly 40 years ago when four U.S. soldiers drowned near Lower Bridge, west of Terrebonne. On Oct. 24, 1943, the soldiers were involved in war-game maneuvers when a boat overturned in swift water, dumping three of the men. A fourth drowned while attempting to save the others. For longtime Bend residents, perhaps the most memorable drowning was that of Frank T. Johns. On May 20, 1928, Johns, a candidate for U.S. president, was campaigning in Drake Park. A Socialist, Johns, 39, was in the middle of a Sunday evening speech when 10-year-old Jack Rhodes fell off the nearby footbridge while fishing and cried for help. Johns flung off his jacket and dove in the icy stream in an attempt to save Rhodes, But while Rhodes' mother and dozens of others looked on, both Johns and the boy drowned. Today a monument in the park pays tribute to Johns for his heroics.

35.4   *Spring River,* only a mile long, is spring-fed, and the source is 1½ miles by canoe from the Sunriver Marina. Explorers who have their own canoes may also put in at Besson Camp, north on the first road past the Sunriver entrance.

36.4   The Deschutes from Besson Camp to Benham Falls Campground is Class I. The river length is 7.5 miles, the shuttle distance is 13.8 miles. To reach put-in, follow above directions to Besson Camp boat ramp. To reach take-out, return to Hwy. 97 and drive north to Lava Lands Visitor Center; turn left at Lava Lands and left again on Rd. 9702. Drive 4 miles to the Benham Falls boat ramp. **You must take out here. Benham Falls would be fatal to attempt.** The portage trail for the falls is on the west side of the Deschutes.

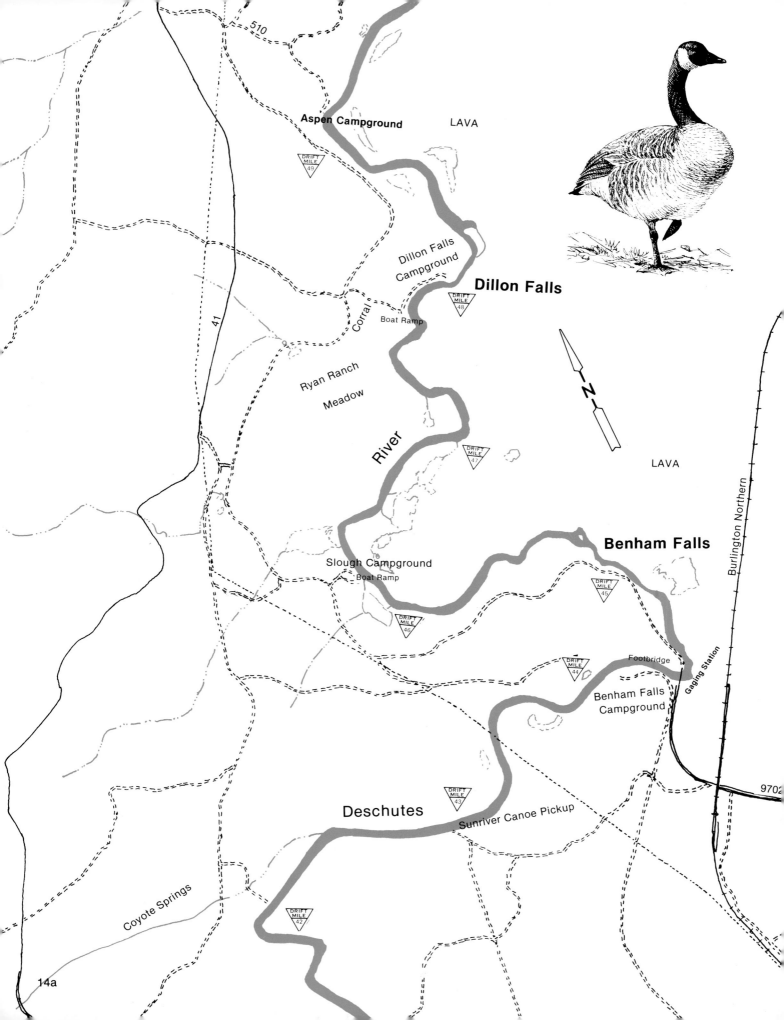

510

Aspen Campground   LAVA

DRIFT MILE 49

Dillon Falls
Campground

Dillon Falls

DRIFT MILE 48

Corral

Boat Ramp

Ryan Ranch

Meadow

River

41

DRIFT MILE 47

N

LAVA

Benham Falls

Slough Campground

Boat Ramp

DRIFT MILE 45

DRIFT MILE 46

Footbridge

DRIFT MILE 44

Gaging Station

Benham Falls
Campground

Burlington Northern

DRIFT MILE 43

Deschutes

Sunriver Canoe Pickup

9702

Coyote Springs

DRIFT MILE 42

14a

Crane Prairie Reservoir was named for this bird. The long-necked wading birds that inhabit the flooded area were the inspiration for the reservoir's name. The Greater Sandhill cranes once nested in a large meadow before a dam was built on the south side, backing up enough water to cover 7 square miles. The meadow has been flooded so often that trees ringing the reservoir are dead and bare.

Courtesy Oregon Department of Fish and Game

Benham Falls

Dillon Falls

Lava Lands

Some 6,000 years ago, a mere minute in geological terms, a large fissure opened in the base of the Newberry volcanic crater. The resulting lava flow covered a massive area now known as Central Oregon's lava lands.

Approximately three miles east of Benham Falls is located the Lava Lands Visitor Center. The center is 10 miles south of Bend off U.S. Highway 97., Visitors can get a good look at the volcanic residue and learn a good deal about the Bend area's geologic past. From the visitors center, a mile-and-a-half drive to the top of Lava Butte offers an even more spectacular view of Oregon's snow capped high country. The road winds to the top of a lava explosion crater, and a walking trail circles the rim of the crater. The Lava River Cave is one mile farther south and a quarter-mile off the highway. Caused by molten rock flowing out from under cooler, hardened lava, much like water running under a frozen stream, the cave is the "longest uncollapsed lava tube in Oregon."

One of the state's most curious lava formations can be found by traveling three and a half miles south from the Lava River Cave on Highway 97, and then following a nine-mile dirt road to the Lava Cast Forest.

When lava spewed from the Newberry Crater it flowed into a grove of evergreens here, massed around the trees and cooled. Burned away by the intense heat of the molten rock, the trees left their molds inside the giant mounds of lava.

Benham Falls

The rapids are named for J.R. Benham. Benham was born in Oregon and moved to Prineville in 1876. Three years later, he moved again to what is now Deschutes County. Benham apparently filed a land claim near the area of the falls in about 1885, but the federal government rejected the claim. Even so, an acquaintance of Benham, Charles Hutchinson, who was in the irrigation business, named the falls after him.

The river was dammed for centuries when lava poured across its 137-foot deep channel at the site of present-day Benham Falls. Before the river could cut a new channel around the barrier and the dam itself was breached, the impounded river filled with silt and fine soil. When the water receded, the soil gave birth to great meadows, which later became the ranches of homesteaders.

With the construction of the railroad, the timber on the Upper Deschutes could be transported to the mills in Bend.

Courtesy Deschutes County Historical Society

The river from Slough Camp to Dillon Falls is Class I. The float is 1.6 miles and the shuttle is little more than 2 miles. To reach put-in, drive past the Inn of the 7th Mountain on Hwy. 46. Turn left at Rd. 41 Jct. (Spring River Rd.; Dillon Falls). Continue on 41 until Dillon Falls sign. Turn left at Dillon Falls sign, drive until you reach Rd. 500. If you go straight through the intersection, you will reach the Dillon Falls take-out. Turn right on Rd. 500 to put in at Slough Camp. **You must take out at Dillon Falls boat ramp; impassable falls directly below.**

Dillon Falls

48.0

The roar of Dillon Falls, one of the mightiest falls along the Deschutes River, can be heard well before one sees it. Tucked into the backwoods south of Bend, the falls is one of the river's most impressive sights. A rather pristine stretch of river before the falls gives no indication of what lies ahead. The water takes a long, twisting plunge over massive, smooth rocks before emptying into another calm stretch of river. A popular sight for anglers, the falls can be reached along a dirt turnoff from the Cascade Lakes Highway, about a half mile west of the Inn of the Seventh Mountain. A fork to the left takes you to the falls.

The falls was named for Leander Dillon, who came with his family from Chico, Calif., in 1885 and homesteaded along the river, where he raised stock. Dillon later lost his land when his claim was denied. He moved to Prineville in 1890.

In 1904 fishing near Benham Falls was excellent.

Courtesy Deschutes County Historical Society

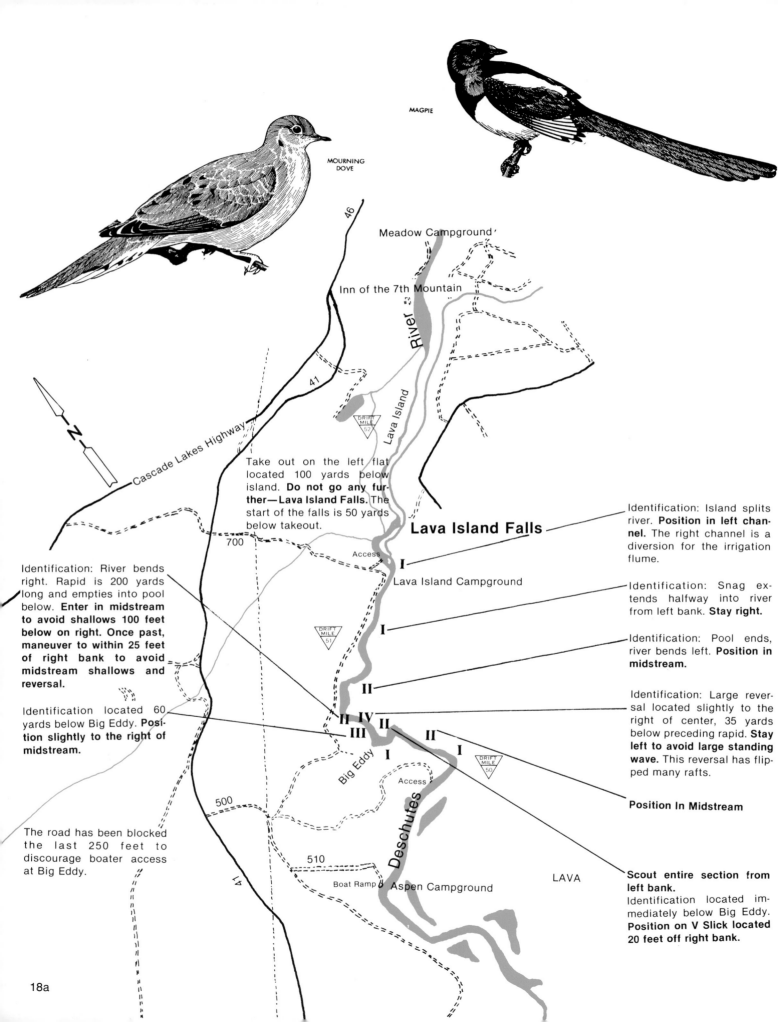

MOURNING DOVE

MAGPIE

Meadow Campground

Inn of the 7th Mountain

River

46

41

Cascade Lakes Highway

Lava Island

DRIFT MILE 52

Take out on the left flat located 100 yards below island. **Do not go any further—Lava Island Falls.** The start of the falls is 50 yards below takeout.

Access

Lava Island Falls

I

Lava Island Campground

700

Identification: Island splits river. **Position in left channel.** The right channel is a diversion for the irrigation flume.

Identification: Snag extends halfway into river from left bank. **Stay right.**

I

DRIFT MILE 51

Identification: River bends right. Rapid is 200 yards long and empties into pool below. **Enter in midstream to avoid shallows 100 feet below on right. Once past, maneuver to within 25 feet of right bank to avoid midstream shallows and reversal.**

Identification: Pool ends, river bends left. **Position in midstream.**

II

Identification: Large reversal located slightly to the right of center, 35 yards below preceding rapid. **Stay left to avoid large standing wave.** This reversal has flipped many rafts.

Identification located 60 yards below Big Eddy. **Position slightly to the right of midstream.**

II IV II

III

I

Big Eddy

Access

II

I

DRIFT MILE 50

Position In Midstream

500

Deschutes

Scout entire section from left bank.

The road has been blocked the last 250 feet to discourage boater access at Big Eddy.

510

Boat Ramp

Aspen Campground

LAVA

Identification located immediately below Big Eddy. **Position on V Slick located 20 feet off right bank.**

41

Big Eddy

Courtesy Hunter Expeditions

The reversal at Big Eddy can flip rafts, but it sure makes good pictures.

Courtesy Hunter Expeditions

49.1

The river from Aspen Camp to Lava Island is Class II & III. Class II to Big Eddy, immediately below Big Eddy there is Class III and IV water. **Take out on left bank to scout Big Eddy.**

The float is 2.7 miles and the shuttle is 2.4 miles. To reach the put-in and take out, turn left off Hwy. 46 onto Rd. 41 (Spring River, Dillon Falls). Turn left onto Rd. 700. The turnoff to the take-out is marked "Lava Island Falls." To reach put-in turn north on Rd. 700 at Lava Island take-out and continue north on Rd. 500 past a confusing intersection. Turn left on Rd. 510 to put in. **You must take out at Lava Island, the falls are directly below.**

The river below Lava Island is not recommended for floating.

51.8

*Prehistoric man habitated the Deschutes near **Lava Island**. In the spring of 1981, two Bend residents found 28 projectile points in the cave, which was used very early in North American prehistory. The find led to a full-scale archaeological investigation by the U.S. Forest Service that summer. The cave, which is relatively small—24 feet across, 3½ feet high and 9 feet deep—yielded artifacts from two other definite time periods.*

Most significant of the artifacts taken from the cave were the large unattached spear points found in the original cache plus five more of the projectiles found 'in place' in the official dig. These distinctive spear points were believed to have been used by nomadic hunters in the area as early as 6,000 to 8,000 B.C. Radiocarbon dating of notched dart points were identified as belonging to a hunting people inhabiting the area from 2,000 B.C. to 1,000 A.D. The presence of primitive knives, cutting and scraping tools and obsidian pieces indicates the people used the cave for the maufacture, repair and storage of their weapons as well as a hunting camp for processing game.

The latest occupation of the cave was traced to the Northern Paiute Indians in 1810 A.D. Small narrow-necked notched projectiles used for the bows and arrows in this much later period were found in the rock shelter. The cave is located five or six miles southwest of Bend on the north end of the island.

Small narrow-necked notched projectiles used for the bows and arrows in this much later period were found in the rock shelter.

The cave is located five or six miles southwest of Bend on the north end of the island.

*The **Bend Bulletin** Wednesday, Jan. 25, 1911.*

52.0

"The Bend Livery Stable recently completed an ice house on the west bank of the Deschutes, near Lava Island, about six miles south of Bend. Last week the men finished putting up about 500 tons of 12-inch ice, and would have put 100 tons more had the weather remained cold. O'Donnell Brothers and Williams Brothers put up about 25 tons of seven inch ice on the river just above the power station.

"In order to secure a suitable pond to cut ice from near Lava Island it was necessary to build a small dam. This backed the water up over the tule swamp, and afforded a comparatively easy place to handle the ice.

"The sawdust to pack the ice in was hauled from the Pilot Butte mill. There is a large supply of it at the Clarke mill, which cut the lumber for the Arnold flume. Although in sight of the new ice house, this sawdust could not be used, as there is no safe bridge over the river between Bend and Lava Island.

"A crew of 17 men and 11 teams were at work constructing the building for about three weeks. The ice house cost $250 and is 30x60 feet and 12 feet high in the clear.

"Besides putting the 500 tons in the ice house, 100 tons were hauled to Bend, Smith & Holmes, the Patterson Drug Co., the Hotel Bend and Dave Biggerstaff storing it for their summer use.

"Last summer ice sold here for $40 a ton. The larger part of it was hauled from the Ice Cave, 12 miles southeast of Bend. The price next summer will be much lower, as the largest consumers have stored a supply that will last most of the summer. They paid $5 per ton for the ice delivered at their storehouses.

"L. L. Fox, who had charge of putting up the ice, stated that the price next summer would not be less than $20 per ton."

LOWER DESCHUTES

If you love whitewater, if you enjoy a challenge, if you live close to nature and if you love the land, you are sure to experience a delightful adventure drifting down the Deschutes river canyon. Lewis and Clark discovered the Deschutes river on October 22, 1805, and first referred to it by its Indian name, *Towornehiooks.* On their return trip, however, they called it Clark's River, presumably for William Clark. The Hudson Bay trappers gave it the name it now bears. In the fur trading period it was known as the Riviere Des Chutes or the Riviere Aux Chutes, meaning River of the Falls. The trappers applied this name because the river flowed into the Columbia near the falls on the Deschutes itself. Presumably, they were referring to the spectacular Celilo Falls of the Columbia, now buried deep below the placid waters of the dammed up river.

The Deschutes offers one of the most enjoyable boat rides in the Northwest. The lower 100 miles of the river is entirely free flowing. It is constantly on the move as the water rushes to meet the Columbia, 13 miles east of The Dalles. The powerful flow maintains an average speed of over 4 miles per hour. The Deschutes drops about 13 feet per mile, a figure comparable to the mighty Colorado as it cuts its path through the Grand Canyon. The whitewater offers a challenge to the seasoned riverman. Whitehorse, Boxcar and several other named rapids start the adrenalin flowing in the most experienced boatmen. These trouble spots have been the sites of fatal accidents and have claimed many boats each year.

Sixty million years ago, much of Oregon and California were under shallow seas. Then the floor of the ocean began to rise and the water gradually drained away into the Pacific Basin. This was followed by the age of mammals, which lasted for several million years. The John Day region has yielded many remains of the "thunder beasts" that ruled the land in ancient times. Fossil remains of rhinoceros, tiny horses, crocodiles, camels and flesh eaters of many types give mute evidence of life in Oregon before the volcanic period spread lava over most of the land, driving out or killing all life.

The Deschutes canyon exhibits spectacular volcanic rock formations. Three of the Cascades' largest volcanoes are located in this area. About 20 million years ago, these volcanoes poured such vast amounts of lava on the surface that mountains over four thousand feet high were buried in basalt. This phenomenon did not occur during a single gigantic eruption, rather the various flows averaged about 30 feet in thickness. Today the central Oregon plateau consists of a hundred flows piled one upon the other. This volcanic activity occurred long before the Cascade Mountains were created.

After the basalt cooled, soil was formed and the unobstructed marine air supplied huge amounts of moisture, creating a rain forest. The land supported such tropical species as teak, ginkgo and cypress. The lush forests also sustained many prehistoric animals, including the huge mastodons. Their remains have been found near Maupin, and in Pleistocene times the animals ranged over central Oregon. There was geological stability for millions of years, then the volcanoes again spewed lava over the land. The new blanket of molten rock entombed all living things, creating petrified forests and rich fossil beds.

A pastor from The Dalles, Thomas Condon, became Oregon's first geologist. Soldiers pursuing Snake Indians discovered fossil remains and Condon had the opportunity to travel into the Deschutes area to collect specimens. He later founded the Geology Department at the University of Oregon.

About 7 million years ago, an enormous uplifting of volcanic rock fashioned the Cascades. The mile high mountain range obstructed the moist Pacific air and created a great desert of basalt in central Oregon. Only a few thousand years ago, ice began to form over the lava plateau. When the mile thick glaciers melted, a flood of gigantic proportions was created. The runoff was a thousand times the magnitude of the great 1964 catastrophe. The incredible force of the melting water scoured and gouged the Deschutes river canyon. The erosion of ancient basalt occurred only yesterday relative to the age of the lava flows.

The river has sliced through the pages of time and opened a window to the past. As you drift down the canyon the flows of lava can be seen to resemble the layers of a cake. Each flow reveals secrets from a prehistoric past.

The Deschutes symbolizes a struggle; a fight for survival. Its location and uniform flow result in this river possessing more hydroelectric potential than any other river in Oregon. In 1964 the Portland General Electric Company completed construction of the Pelton-Round Butte Hydroelectric Project. At one time or another dams have been proposed at many sites along the entire length of the river.

The source of the Deschutes river is Lava Lake, near the mountain called the south Sister. As it flows north to the Columbia, the river resembles a tree with nearly all the branches on one side. Except for Crooked River and Trout Creek, all its feeder streams originate in the Cascades and enter from the west. It is a river of remarkably even flow year round. During the period of heavy runoff, the excess water is impounded in the spongy lava bed so the river level at Bend is essentially the same at all seasons. H.A. Tetherow used to operate a ferry on the river and he stated that in sixteen years the level never varied over sixteen inches.

Crooked River originates seventy-five miles southeast of its union with the Deschutes, and is by far the largest tributary from the east. It arises from large springs in the Ochoco Mountains and it flows into the Deschutes, not far above where the Metolius enters from the west. The Metolius is also a river arising from large springs below Three Fingered Jack.

At one time, lava flowed into the Crooked River Canyon in the locality of Smith Rock. The lava completely filled the gorge and continued its flow downstream, choking the confluence of the Deschutes and Crooked Rivers with a "plug" about eight hundred feet high. The two rivers cut their present gorges through the blockading lava. This is the spectacular "Cove Island," the landmark known to the pioneers as "The Plains of Abraham," grandly visible from the Cove Palisades State Park.

The first white men into the Deschutes area were trappers from the Hudson Bay Company. In December, 1825, two parties met along the banks of the river near Metolius. One group, led by Peter Skene Ogden, ascended from the Columbia and the other group, led by Finan McDonald, crossed the Cascades from the west. From here they moved up the Crooked River, finding a few beaver but not

Peter Skene Ogden was the first white man to visit this area.

enough game to feed the men. They had to butcher several of their horses to keep from starving and finally passed over the divide into the John Day area.

The following year, Ogden made another trip into central Oregon. On this trip the party attempted to cross the river at Sherars Falls on an Indian fishing platform located there. Five horses broke through the span and fell into the rapids below.

In 1834 Nathaniel J. Wyeth became the first to explore south of the Crooked River and to visit the present site of Bend. Historian Hubert Howe Bancroft said of him: "He it was who, more directly than anyone else, marked the way for the oxteams which were shortly to bring civilization from the east."

In 1843 the Army sent John C. Fremont to explore the west. The assignment was obtained with the help of his father-in-law, Senator Thomas Benton. Fremont started out of The Dalles in November, 1843, and followed the Deschutes to its headwaters and then to the Klamath Marsh and eventually into California. His guide was Kit Carson.

In 1845 the first wagon train crossed central Oregon. It was called the Bluebucket Mine Party. It left the main Oregon Trail near Fort Boise and started across the plains, guided by Stephen Meek, on a route later known as the Meek Cutoff. Somewhere along the way, children sent to get water in a blue bucket came back with gold nuggets in the bottom of the bucket. The nuggets were not noticed for several days and the lode has never been located, although folks are still looking. Further on, the train became lost and thirst and starvation resulted in many deaths. They were finally rescued by a search party from The Dalles.

The second immigrant train to cross central Oregon was a small family group known as the Clark Massacre Party. The name derives from an Indian attack on the Snake River, in which several members of the party were killed. Following the attack, they made an uneventful crossing.

The Elliott Cutoff Party, in 1853, was a large group of 250 wagons and over 1,000 persons who tried to find a pass across the Cascades, along the middle fork of the Willamette. They became lost, not knowing one landmark from another, and suffered severe hardships before finally being found and rescued by people from Lane County.

Paulina.

WARM SPRINGS RESERVATION

The Warm Springs Reservation was created by the Treaty of 1855 for the Confederated Tribes and Bands of central Oregon. The confederation includes Walla Wallas, Wascos and Paiutes. The Walla Wallas are now known as the Warm Springs Tribe.

More specifically, these bands included the Taih or upper Deschutes band of Walla Wallas, the Wyam or lower Deschutes band of Walla Wallas, the Tenino band of Walla Wallas, the Dock-spus or John Day band of Walla Wallas, The Dalles band of Wascos, the Ki-Gal-Twal-La band of Wascos, and the Dog River band of Wascos. The third tribe residing on the reservation are the Paiutes. They were placed there after the campaigns against them between 1866 and 1868. The Paiutes are a branch of the Snakes, living in the Malheur area. In this campaign by General Crook, two-thirds of the Paiutes were killed and the remainder reduced to starvation and then placed on the Warm Springs Reserve.

Howard Maupin.

The Indian of most historic interest in the Deschutes area was a renegade chief known as Paulina. He was a Snake Indian sometimes called "Bulletproof" Paulina. His many escapes from local troops earned him the name of "Atilla of the Sagelands." He was given to raiding ranches and stealing cattle.

Soldiers and volunteers made several unsuccessful attempts to capture or kill him. They were aided by scouts from the Warm Springs Reservation. These people had good reason for aiding the whites, inasmuch as Paulina frequently raided their reservation, taking captives and stealing horses. In 1866, Paulina and his band attacked and killed the Reservation chief who was on a hunting expedition.

His final episode came after he had driven off a herd of cattle from a John Day ranch and crossed the divide near the headwaters of Crooked River. A local rancher, Howard Maupin, located the Indians breakfasting on a butchered steer. When the shooting stopped, Paulina was dead and his skeleton was left to bleach in the sun for many years where he had fallen. Despite his evil reputation, or perhaps because of it, Paulina's name has been bestowed on more central Oregon places than any other individual's. A lake, a mountain, a town, a prairie, a peak, and a creek all bear the name of Paulina. The town

of Maupin was named for Howard Maupin, who after killing Paulina, subsequently operated a ferry at that site.

Despite the tide of immigrants crossing central Oregon on their way to the Columbia and Willamette Valleys, none of them settled in the interior until after 1863. Except for a few venturesome miners, and those tending the ferries and fords, the land was devoid of settlers, chiefly due to Indians.

In 1856, General Wool issued an order forbidding immigrants to locate east of the Cascades. This mandate was justified as "a most valuable separation of the two races." In 1858, however, General Harney revoked the order when it became apparent that it would be more difficult to keep the whites out of that region than to keep the Indians under control.

The Homestead Law of 1862 allowed a U.S. Citizen to acquire 160 acres of public domain, but many who took up such lands found there was no water with which to grow crops. Later, this area became the locale of very large cattle ranches, to be followed by the influx of sheep ranches. Both competed for the pasture land and mountain summer range, leading to inevitable range wars.

Early day travelers stop at a springs near Sherars bridge.

Cattlemen formed groups called Sheep Shooters, such as the IZEE Sheep Shooters, and later the Crook County Sheep Shooting Association. These groups did exactly as the name implied. The greatest of all sheep slaughters took place at Benjamin Lake near the Crook-Lake County line in 1903. 2,400 sheep were shot after the herder and the camp tender were bound and blindfolded. In 1904 several such slaughters were carried out around Silver Lake. In 1905 and 1906 similar episodes occurred. Finally, these activities were brought to a halt by federal forest supervisors who began to assign grazing permits to all parties, each with allotted specific boundaries.

RULE OF THE VIGILANTES

In March, 1882, two men were killed near Prineville in a property line dispute that led to two years of rule by self-styled vigilantes. It started when the two men, A.H. Crooks and his son-in-law S.J. Jory, were working on a line fence and were apparently shot by a neighbor, Lucius Langdon. A loosely organized posse was formed in Prineville and Langdon and an employee of his, W.H. Harrison, were arrested and a deputy sheriff was assigned to guard him. During the night the guard was overpowered by a mob of masked men. Langdon was shot and killed and Harrison was dragged through the streets behind a galloping horse and then hung from a bridge at the end of town. This act became even more tragic after it had been established that Harrison was in Prineville at the time of the murders and could not have been a participant.

Out of these events grew the Crook County Vigilantes, who enforced their own laws for a two year period, during which nine men were killed. Eventually, the more stable men of the area revolted against this rule and formed their own group, known as the Moonshiners. When the newly formed Crook County held its first elections in 1884, practically all those who opposed the vigilantes were elected, and regular law and order again prevailed. It should be stated in this regard that, up to this time, the area was all part of Wasco County, with a sheriff located in The Dalles. The only officer in central Oregon was one deputy sheriff.

RAILROAD BATTLE OF THE GORGE

As early as 1855, the possibility of building a railroad into central Oregon was being considered. The Deschutes Canyon was explored by the U.S. Army Topographic Engineers in 1855, who reported that it would be impossible to build a railroad up the narrow rock-walled gorge.

Later railroaders were not so easily discouraged, and over the years many railroads were planned on paper, some going east to west and others north to south. None of these were ever actually built, however, until a branch line was built from the Columbia into Shaniko in 1900.

The prize for building a successful railroad into this area proved ultimately to be irresistable. In addition to the cattle and sheep, there were sixteen billion board feet of pine growing on the slopes of the Cascades and the Ochoco Mountains. Equally important to James J. Hill of the Great Northern, was the fact that once he could get his railroad to Bend, he would be in a position to continue on south to California.

In 1906 the company called the Oregon Trunk Line was formed and surveyed a route up the Deschutes Canyon to Madras. In 1907 another company, the Des Chutes Railroad, made and filed similar maps. Although essentially unrecognized at the time, this was the beginning of a monumental multi-million dollar struggle between two great barons of the railroad world; the "empire builder," James J. Hill, of the Great Northern, and Edward H. Harriman of the Union Pacific and Southern Pacific.

The Oregon Trunk Line was a Hill subsidiary, while the Des Chutes Railroad was controlled by Harriman. No construction was begun in 1908, but in that year a very important legal maneuver was accomplished by the Hill forces. A new company, the Central Oregon Railroad, was then purchased by the Oregon Trunk Line. By thus acquiring this vital site for crossing the Crooked River Canyon, Hill virtually blocked the Harriman attempt to build a parallel line to Bend.

Construction work began in 1909, the Des Chutes Railroad built on the east bank of the river, while the Hill interests kept their crews on the west bank. It was not a friendly race, each side using legal and physical means as necessary to interfere with the other's progress. Gunshots were occasionally exchanged. Landslides occurred at opportune times, and a favorite trick was to locate and destroy the opponent's powder caches, thus forcing delays.

Each side spent between twenty-five and thirty million dollars. Labor forces numbered three to four thousand on each side and were largely emigrants from southern Europe. Common laborers were paid twenty to thirty cents per hour while skilled laborers commanded thirty-five to forty cents per hour. This spectacular feat marked the end of an era, being one of the last big jobs virtually "done by hand." It seems incredible now that this work was done with picks, shovels, wheelbarrows, hand drills and black powder.

Although many difficulties were avoided by the agreement that the Union Pacific (Harriman system) hold to the east bank and the Oregon Trunk stay on the west side, some conflict still developed. One incident occurred in the area of the Warm Springs Indian Reservation, where the Oregon Trunk had no right-of-way. So, Hill built a grade across the Des Chutes Railroad survey line at Mile 75, blocking the Harriman crews. At approximately the same time, the Des Chutes Railroad obtained title to a homestead in the North Junction area which effectively blocked the Oregon Trunk.

The government finally settled these matters by enforcing what was known as the Canyon Act, whereby a compromise was effected. Both sides agreed to a joint track usage, covering eleven miles between what became known as North Junction and South Junction.

Early in the gorge struggle, the Oregon Trunk Line began work on the road from Madras to Bend and on the bridge across Crooked River. The Harriman people (Harriman died in 1909) entered into various agreements with the Hill system so that they obtained joint usage of the Oregon Trunk Line from Metolius to Bend.

On October 5, 1911, "empire builder" James J. Hill, drove the golden spike at the end of the rails in Bend. Not one but two railroads had been completed up the "impossible gorge."

Gradually, over the years, the Oregon Trunk and the Union Pacific consolidated trackage in the Deschutes Gorge. By mid-century, both lines operated over a single track and most of the Des Chutes Railroad grade has been converted into an automobile access road which follows the lower Deschutes river.

"The Empire Builder," James J. Hill.

Edward H. Harriman of the Union Pacific Railroad.

These heavy timbers were used to build bridges and trestles for both railroads.

These railroad construction men pause to rest after a long, hot day in the summer of 1909.

HARRY E. CARLETON, CONTRACTOR

The railroad construction era involved thousands of men. They came from all walks of life and many nations, searching for wealth and adventure. They entered the steep walled canyon with uncertainty, knowing that some would never return.

Railroad barons Hill and Harriman have always been linked to the last great railroad war which was fought here in the Deschutes canyon. However, few are familiar with the names of the contractors who actually built the railroads. An example of one such contractor was Harry E. Carleton.

Before the age of 30, Harry had established his reputation as a heavy construction contractor and tunnel builder. He and his faithful crew of Italian laborers had just completed a railroad job in the Bitterroot Mountains of Montana. While Harry was enjoying the Seattle World's Fair in the summer of 1909, he received a message from his friend, Johnson Porter, urgently requesting his assistance to construct a railroad up the Deschutes river canyon. The Porter Brothers construction firm had secured a contract from the Great Northern Railroad to build a railroad from the Columbia river, up the

Deschutes gorge to Bend. Upon receiving this information, Harry packed his bags and headed for Portland, not realizing he would play a major role in the last great railroad war.

In 1906, the Porter brothers were assigned to conduct a preliminary survey along the east bank of the Deschutes river, from the Columbia to Madras. In 1909, the Twohy Brothers Construction Company (contracted by the Union Pacific Railroad) jumped the Great Northern survey, and began to build a railroad for the Union Pacific. This maneuver stimulated the Great Northern Railway (which owned the Oregon Trunk) to appoint the Porter Brothers Construction Company to regain the original survey right of way. The stage was set for the last great battle.

Carleton arrived in Portland for his meeting with Johnson Porter. Upon completion of Harry's briefing, Porter summarized the situation by saying, "We're going to have to organize an army and go in there and take the Union Pacific bunch out."

Harry's first move was to contact the men he

Harry Carleton checks construction of wooden bridge at "Twin Crossings" tunnel.

Engineers' camp for the Oregon Trunk. Island at Harris Canyon, flooded in the Spring of 1910.

knew best. They were all Italians and had come to the United States to work on railroad construction. They planned to return to their homeland, and Harry would send their earnings to their families after each payday. They had learned to trust the Irishman, and called him "Carletoni."

Within a few days, approximately 100 men had been organized by Harry. The entire crew boarded a paddle wheeler in Portland and headed up the Columbia to The Dalles. They arrived late that afternoon and camped on the beach. The next morning, Harry's "army" had grown to 150 men. He gathered their supplies into three 4-horse wagons and the robust crew headed for Freebridge, to cross the Deschutes on the way to their new headquarters at Grass Valley.

As they left The Dalles, the outfit took the wrong road and ended up in the small hamlet of Boyd late on a hot June night. Harry recalled the citizens of Boyd were quite upset. In those early days there was no communication as we know it today, and the local townspeople were shocked by the unexpected arrival of 150 "foreigners." The group camped in a vacant lot across from the general store. There was whooping and hollering around the big bonfires as the young men sang native songs

and caroused all night. The town pump squeaked and squealed as the exhausted men tried to quench their thirst. Frightened townspeople barred their doors and loaded their shotguns as they prepared for the worst. However, the next morning they were relieved to see the stalwart group head out of town.

Carleton and his crew crossed at Freebridge and climbed to the east plateau. When they reached the head of Harris canyon, which the Twohy Brothers' outfit had made passable to supply their construction crews below, they met armed guards. The sentries denied Carleton's crew passage down Harris grade, and Carleton offered no resistance — at least not in the daylight. However, as soon as darkness fell, Carleton's men headed into the rugged canyon. As the three 4-horse wagons and 150 armed Italians cautiously descended the steep grade in total darkness, gunfire met them from the crew below. Harry's men retaliated and suddenly the canyon walls were illuminated with gunfire. Luckily, there were no serious injuries and Carleton's crew was able to take possession of a small flat on the river's edge. They set up camp that night and awaited dawn.

The stalemate persisted for three weeks. Hostilities were magnified as the two rival groups mingled

These engineers were responsible for surveying much of the lower Deschutes Canyon.

with each other on the small campsite. Every day, Sheriff Freeman arrived with three or four deputies. His presence calmed the jumpy men and preserved a semblance of order. Freeman did not permit his law enforcement officers to carry firearms, and this was probably the most important factor in preventing bloodshed in the camp.

The next move was made by the Oregon Trunk. Johnson Porter arranged to purchase the Fred Girt ranch, a strategically located homestead at the head of Harris grade. The new road built by the Twohy Brothers allowed access to the Deschutes canyon through the ranch and, in their haste to begin construction, they had overlooked the possibility that the rival company could buy the land on which the road was built. By controlling the access, it was possible to shut off the supply route to the Union Pacific construction crews located below.

Once the transaction was complete, the road was fenced off and 75 men under the direction of Harry Carleton moved in to blockade the entrance to Harris grade, in a deliberate move to starve out the Union Pacific work force. The blockade was successful. Stranded supply wagons were backed up single file along the road, unable to reach the men below the high plateau. After several days, Sheriff Freeman and his posse appeared with Judge Littlefield. The lawmen were accompanied by newspaper reporters, including the *Oregonian's* George Putnam (who later married aviatrix Amelia Earhart). Obviously, history was about to be made, and an early day moving picture machine had been carefully trundled across the dry desert to record what happened next.

The judge demanded to know who was in charge. Carleton replied, "I guess I am."

"Well, I'm going to open this gate," Littleton stated. By this time there were eight 4-horse teams and one pack outfit waiting to pass down the grade.

"I've got orders from headquarters not to let anyone go through," replied Carleton.

"And I'm ordering you that they *will* go through. I have an order from the court. I'm going to open that gate," pronounced Littlefield. He untwisted a piece of wire and the gate was down.

"What are you going to do about that?" barked Littlefield.

"I'm not going to do anything while you open the gate, but you're still not going through," murmured Carleton. "I've got to obey orders, same as anybody else."

All tunnel construction at the "Twin Crossings" was done by hand.

"Well, we'll see about that," replied Littlefield. The judge then beckoned to the first 4-horse team to come ahead. The team started up and then all hell broke loose.

In Carleton's own words: "I gave orders to my men to stop the team, and right then I lost control of the whole layout. Not being the army, why the next thing I knew, the Italians had piled all over everything. They pulled Freeman and his deputies off their horses; the judge was bounced around in the dust and was just completely wild-eyed; and the Italians, instead of just stopping the team from going through the gate, unhitched the horses and pulled the harnesses off. There were horses running wild all through the sagebrush. After a while things quieted down and the judge walked up to me and shook his hand and said, 'I'm going to see that you're indicted for inciting a riot!' and then, besides that, Sheriff Freeman walked up and placed me under arrest. I said, 'Well, I guess I have to obey the law, but still nobody's going through the gate.'"

Fortunately, Johnson Porter arrived before things got worse, and ordered the gate opened. The blockade had served its purpose. The maneuver had attracted enough attention to force the U.S. District Court to assign each competing railroad one bank of the Deschutes river for its construction work. The Union Pacific was restricted to the east side, and the Oregon Trunk was confined to the west. The decision was welcomed by the Porter Brothers because the west bank was far superior for railroad construction.

Once the right of way was settled, the two railroads began a frantic race to Bend. Thousands of men in a hundred strategically located camps began to work simultaneously at midnight, July 26, 1909. On October 5, 1911, James Hill drove the golden spike of the Oregon Trunk at Bend.

Harry Carleton was just one of some twenty subcontractors who worked under the direction of the Porter Brothers construction company. Carleton received the contract to build the 12-mile section of track which extends from the mouth of White River downstream to a point near Oak Canyon on the west bank. The present tunnel at Twin Bridges (drift mile 56.4) was built by the Carleton crew. It serves as a constant reminder of a great man, his Italian "army" and the end of a railroad era.

EXPLANATION OF WHITEWATER CLASSIFICATIONS
OR
"DEGREE OF DIFFICULTY"

General Comments: The rapids which you will encounter on your journey down the Deschutes range in difficulty from very simple to very complicated. An effort to evaluate each rapid has been made to classify them by their "degree of difficulty." Minor rapids consist of Types 1 and 2; major rapids consist of Types 3 or greater. As a general rule, it is advisable to scout all Type 3 rapids (and all with higher degrees of difficulty) BEFORE entering.

EXPLANATIONS OF "DEGREES OF DIFFICULTY"

TYPE 1   Easy. Offers no major obstructions. Water surface shows only small riffles. Low hydraulic forces are in effect. No significant danger other than the simple, unobstructed force of the current of the river. The majority of the rapids on the lower 100 miles of the Deschutes fall into this category.

TYPE 2   Medium difficulty. Streamflow increases in velocity. Obstructions may necessitate some maneuvering. Medium hydraulics will be experienced. Small standing waves or relatively safe medium-sized standing waves are possible.

TYPE 3   DANGEROUS. Swamping or overturning is common. Medium to high streamflow velocities will be encountered. Standing waves will be present. Powerful hydraulics exist. Maneuvering will be required during passage. Dangerous suckholes may form at large boulders. Midstream obstructions may be present. Novices should seriously consider lining their boats through these rapids.

TYPE 4   VERY DANGEROUS. Extended rapids necessitate long-term difficulties. High standing waves and midstream obstructions force maneuvering in powerful hydraulics. Suckholes are capable of capsizing the most stable craft. Novices should not attempt. Novices should line boats through these rapids or portage around them.

TYPE 5   EXTREMELY DANGEROUS. These rapids require technical maneuvering in strong hydraulics. Rapids may be extended for some distance. Standing waves and midstream obstructions or suckholes present serious hazards to equipment and life. Novices and many experienced boatmen should line boats through or portage around.

TYPE 6   FOOLISH TO ATTEMPT. Involves life hazard. Waterfalls, impossible hydraulics and necessary maneuvering combine to make safe passage more a matter of luck than skill. Lining boats through or portaging around is recommended for even the most competent boatmen.

Salvage expert Mark Angel brings them back up as fast as Whitehorse can swallow them down.

These rafters did not realize that they were at Boxcar until it was too late.

BOATING SAFETY

Before starting down the river you must know your limitations and abilities. Your age, physical condition and experience should all enter into your decisions. Never overload your boat so that it cannot be turned quickly and easily maneuvered. Load the boat with the heavy objects near the bottom to keep the center of gravity at its lowest point (to reduce the likelihood of swamping). After properly loading the boat, securely tie down all objects in the boat to prevent weight shift. Make sure the boat, including gear and passengers, is balanced perfectly before entering any section of the river which necessitates maneuvering. Assign specific positions to passengers to prevent loss of balance. Be sure you and your passengers know what to expect from each other during emergencies. Passengers must have their lifejackets on and securely fastened. Once started down the river you cannot backtrack easily, and help may be many miles away. Don't take chances. Any rapids which cannot be clearly seen ahead should be scouted before entering. Pull ashore upstream and evaluate the rapids carefully. Predetermine your route through the rapids before returning to your boat. Never be overconfident in any rapids no matter how small they may seem. The least obvious factor can cause extreme difficulties at any time. It is important to realize that hazards vary with the river level — during high water, standing waves may appear, creating impassable suckholes and back-eddies. Sometimes a new course will have to be found. When passing through whitewater, the passengers should be assigned specific parts of the boat to grasp to prevent uncontrolled weight shifts. Never get broadside to the current in fast water. If you see that you are going to hit an obstruction, NEVER hit it broadside, ALWAYS hit it head on. Always counterbalance the boat when striking an object — this can be accomplished by shifting the weight to the "high" side (the opposite side to which the boat is leaning). This should be practiced before your journey begins. Don't wait until an emergency to find out that your passenger doesn't know how to counterbalance! Steer clear of overhanging branches and all submerged objects. The current's force is much stronger than you are, and it must be respected at all times. It can cause serious injuries and accidents. Don't overexert your physical capacities. Don't try to float too far in a single day. Fatigue sets in slowly and may weaken you when you need maximum strength and alertness.

Your craft should be outfitted with the following essential pieces of equipment: one 100 ft. lining rope (for lining your boat around falls, severe rapids, and nighttime securing when fastenings are some distance from the river), adequate rope for tie-downs to secure your equipment inside your craft (we start with four 25 ft. lengths of ¼ inch rope, which can be either cut into shorter pieces or tied together to make a second 100 ft. rope for emergency situations), two extra oars or paddles (oars and paddles break — sometimes in the middle of rapids). Position one spare oar or paddle on either side of your craft, readily available in case of emergency. Also, remember two extra oarlocks (oarlocks may break or be lost by accident, and they don't float), a boat repair kit suited to repair your type of craft, a plastic bailing bucket (to conform to the bottom of your craft more readily) and we recommend Type 1 Personal Flotation Devices for safety's sake.

Check your boat before your journey. Be sure it is in good physical condition. Make sure wooden boats do not have dry rot; fiberglass boats should not be cracked or leaking; rubber boats should not have leaks or cracks and the rubber should be in good shape. Be certain that the blocks that hold the oarlocks in place are not cracked or split and are securely attached to the frame of the boat — all the stress of the rapids will be transmitted through these sensitive areas and they are the primary source of problems when accidents occur on rivers.

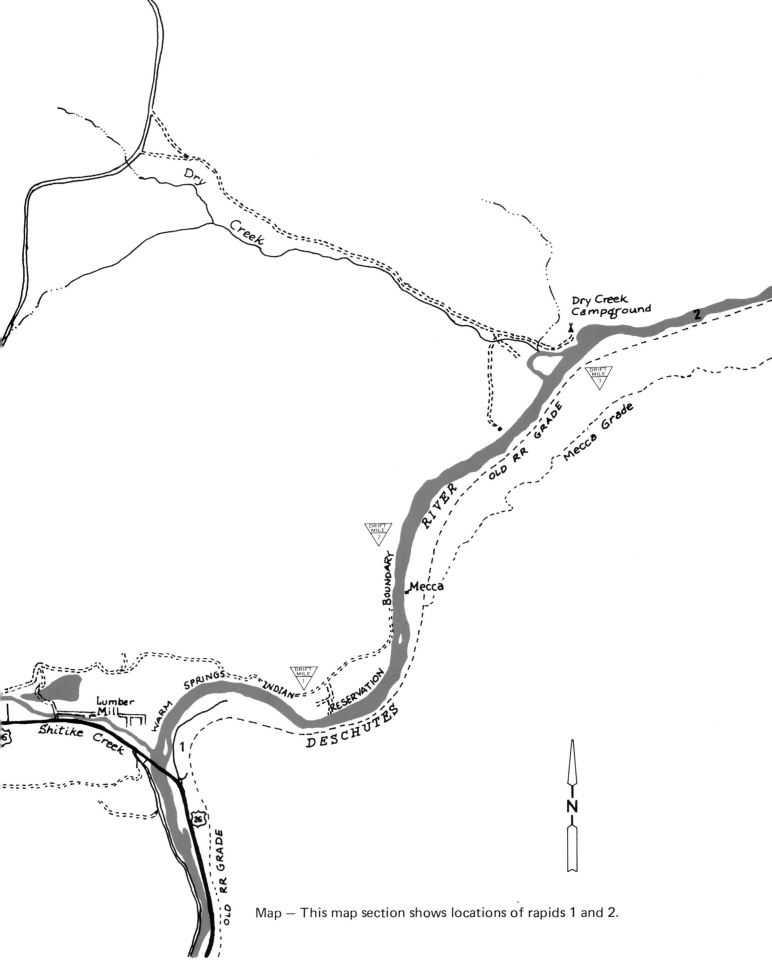

Map — This map section shows locations of rapids 1 and 2.

Aerial view of Warm Springs and boat ramp. Note old abandoned Oregon Trunk Railroad tunnel now used to store potatoes (upper right).

—   0.0   —   PREPARATION: The upper boat ramp is located on the east bank of the Deschutes River. It is approximately 300 yards upstream from the Warm Springs bridge. This site was once a fruit orchard, called Cole Island. The original channel between the island and the east bank has been filled so that you can reach the ramp. The Fish and Wildlife Commission maintains the launching ramp and posts current regulations and safety warnings next to the ramp itself. Although outdoor fire pits permit overnight camping, there are no toilet or water facilities and wood is scarce. A small grocery store across the highway has a good supply of last minute supplies.

COMMENTS: The gradient of the Deschutes River is fairly uniform between this launching site and its junction with the Columbia River, 97 miles downstream. The average drop is 13 feet per mile, and the average current speed is 4 miles per hour. By calculating the current speed, and coordinating it with your day's activities, you should be able to arrive at your evening camp with enough time to prepare for the evening hours in comfort. The Deschutes River is the eastern boundary of the Warm Springs Indian Reservation. This reservation land remains on your left for the first 28 miles of your downriver journey. The remains of an old roadbed are still visible. This grade permitted travel between Warm Springs and the trading post located at Mecca. Once you have launched your vessel, you will drift some 300 yards downstream to pass under the Warm Springs bridge. Pass under the bridge on the right side. Within 50 feet you will see Shitike Creek entering the river from the left side. The name "shitike" is derived from the Klamath term "Sidaikti" which indicated the general locality of the Warm Springs reservation area in the days before the reservation was established. Pioneer settlers found the natural delta suitable for their first buildings when the town of Warm Springs was first settled. About 150 yards downstream on the right bank below the Warm Springs Bridge, the concrete portal of the old Oregon Trunk railway tunnel No. 5 is seen. Today it is used as a root cellar to store potatoes.

Kitchen Kamp seat used in a raft for seating.

And the Kitchen Kamp seat used in camp for kitchen duty.

Rapid No.	Mileage	Class	
1	0.3	1	**IDENTIFICATION:** Shitike Creek enters the river on the left side, approximately 50 yards above the whitewater riffle.

HOW TO: Pass through on the right side of the river, approximately 1/3 off the right bank.

COMMENTS: The Warm Springs Federation of Indian Tribes owns and operates the sawmill which you can see in operation on the left bank. Ahead, about 200 yards, identify a small midstream island tufted with grass. The right channel is whitewater, but the left channel is clear. Pass to the left. Another 500 yards downstream you will see 2 modern homes on the right bank, and directly across the river, on the left bank, you can see the remains of an old wooden irrigation trough. Gravity was used in early days to bring water from higher levels, such as the upstream reaches of the river or supply creeks. The water was used to irrigate the lower plains which you will pass as you continue your journey downstream.

| — | 1.0 | — | |

COMMENTS: At this point you can look back upstream and see Mount Jefferson. This is the last view of the Cascades that you will see. The large flat on the west side was used as an agricultural area, but today modern homes are present. On one trip, a member of our party was bitten by a rattlesnake when he walked a short distance along this flat. Also, on the right bank, you can identify the remains of the old Oregon Trunk railroad grade running about 50 feet above river level parallel with the river.

| — | 1.5 | — | |

COMMENTS: The Oregon Trunk railroad abandoned this route in 1923. As you continue downstream, you will come to a midstream island which marks the beginning of the flat at "Mecca" (on the right). Mecca was a station for the Oregon Trunk railroad line. Railroad builders found their labors so difficult as they built the tracks through the Deschutes canyon upstream from the Columbia River, that they longed for an end to the difficulties that beset them. They came to think of this flat as their longed-for "Mecca" because it marked the end of the most difficult segment of their upriver toils. The old wagon road from Madras to Warm Springs Agency came down from Agency Plain (on the east side). The grade was very steep and dangerous. Its remains can still be seen in the distance, carved into the hillsides. This old wagon road used to cross the river here at Mecca, and you will pass by the original concrete pier structures of the bridge which was used. The Post Office and general store at Mecca were discontinued when a new highway following Willow Creek was built. The Warm Springs bridge replaced the old wagon road bridge which used to cross here.

| — | 2.0 | — | |

COMMENTS: For the next mile or more you can identify the rock structure which was the bed of an old road running along the left bank. This road bed will follow the Deschutes River until we near the mouth of Dry Creek ahead, at which time it will turn west to follow Dry Creek out of the Deschutes canyon and reach the high plateaus above you.

Look who dropped in for dinner.

Photo by Don Turcke

Oregon Trunk Railroad leaves Deschutes Canyon at Trout Creek.

Rapid No.	Mileage	Class	
—	3.0	—	COMMENTS: *Dry Creek enters the Deschutes River on the left side. An old ranch is located upriver a short distance from Dry Creek's junction with the river. Dry Creek Flat is of interest because it was here that Peter Skene Ogden spent several days before fording the Deschutes River in the winter of 1825. Ogden was the first white explorer to journey through this area. In 1843 another famous explorer, John C. Fremont, also camped here. Fremont was accompanied by the renowned frontier guide Kit Carson, and Indian guide Billy Chinook (an Indian chief of renown). A large campsite is on the left bank, approximately 100 yards downstream from the creek. If you wish, you may obtain a special fishing permit from the Confederated Tribes in Warm Springs. With this permit, you may fish along the west bank for approximately the next 8 miles. Across from the Dry Creek campground, on the right bank, a home is built on another small flat. Notice the characteristic poplar tree planting, which helps control wind and water erosion.*
2	3.5	1	IDENTIFICATION: A small campground is located on the right bank, with a sandy area, a park bench and a garbage can. The riffle itself is very small and easy. A cave can be seen on the right bank hillside about 100 yards from river level. This is private property, camping is not allowed. **HOW TO: Pass through in midstream.**
3	3.8	1	IDENTIFICATION: Approximately 200 yards downstream from No. 2. **HOW TO: Pass through in midstream.**
4	4.0	1	IDENTIFICATION: River splits around a midstream island, mainstream is to the left. **HOW TO: Stay in left channel to pass this gentle riffle in midchannel.** COMMENTS: *A small campsite can be seen on the right bank, about 250 yards below No. 4. It has a toilet and garbage can. The fence marks the beginning of public land. Be sure to camp on the downstream side of it.*
5	4.4	1	IDENTIFICATION: A small island is on the left side of the river at the beginning of this piece of whitewater. Located approximately 350 yards downstream from No. 4. **HOW TO: Stay midstream to pass through with no trouble.**
6	4.7	1	IDENTIFICATION: Midstream shallowing forms small standing waves. A campsite is located on right bank in midriffle. **HOW TO: Pass through in midstream with no trouble.**
7	5.3	1	IDENTIFICATION: Stangland Island Riffle — the river passes around Stangland Island. Main channel is to the left. **HOW TO: Stay to the left, and pass through in midstream.** COMMENTS: *Camping is not permitted on any island. All have been posted by the B.L.M. and Warm Springs Confederated Tribes. A campsite is located on the right bank of the river, adjacent to the downstream end of the island. As you continue downstream several hundred yards, basalt cliffs form 300-foot walls on the left riverbank. About 500 yards below No. 7, an interesting formation of columnar basalt can be seen near river level on the left bank. This is an interesting view of a classic geologic rock formation.*

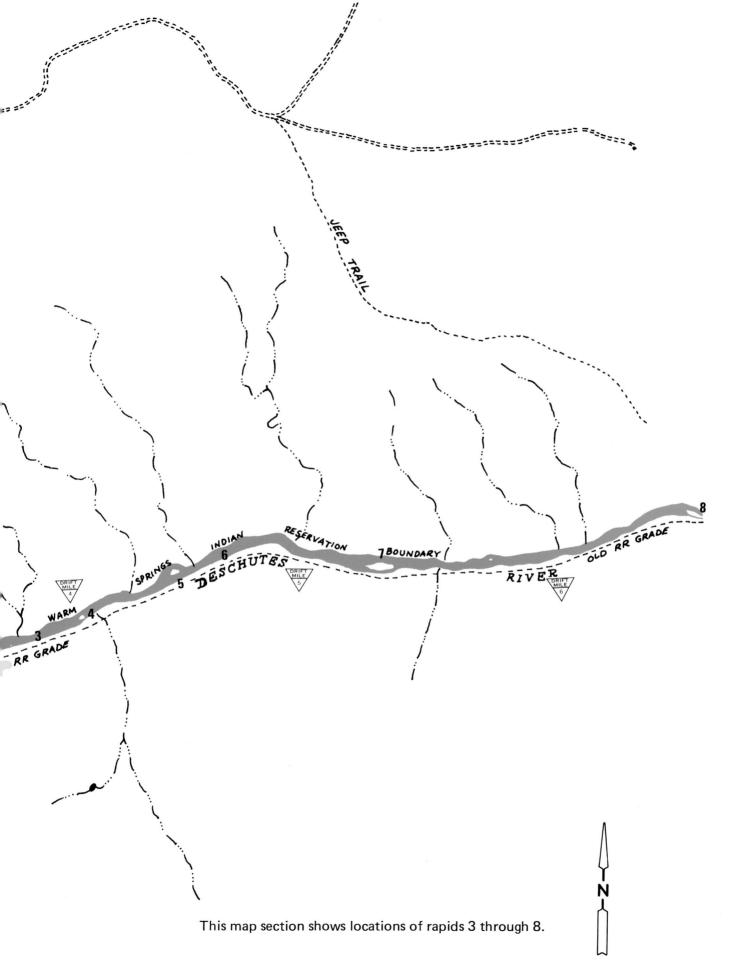

This map section shows locations of rapids 3 through 8.

N

Rapid No.	Mileage	Class
—	6.0	—

COMMENTS: *On the right bank you will see the first examples of rocky basalt cliffs covered with green lichen. Also, watch for a small campsite on the right.*

8	6.7	1

IDENTIFICATION: An island splits the river almost equally. Grass and small alders grow on the island. The left channel is the easier route.

HOW TO: Remain in midchannel, either side. Avoid small obstacles.

COMMENTS: *A campground is located on the right bank, just below the island. Toilet available. A footbridge crosses Frog Springs Creek at the level of the old railroad grade.*

9	6.9	1

IDENTIFICATION: Approximately 100 yards below the campground described above, the river bends left and water forms a minor chop as it curves.

HOW TO: Stay midstream for simple passage.

COMMENTS: *The river continues in a long bend to the left. The large eddy is called "Indian Hole." A campsite with toilet and garbage can is located on the right bank a short distance ahead.*

10	7.4	1

IDENTIFICATION: Midstream standing waves; river bends to the right at the bottom of the standing waves. Whitewater continues around S-turn in the river ahead.

HOW TO: Stay midstream, riding on crests of standing waves. Avoid shallows on left side of river.

COMMENTS: *These are the first standing waves of any consequence which you have met on your journey downriver. Our suggestion is to ride the crests of these smaller standing waves to obtain quickest passage (and most fun!) Riding the crests has the advantage of avoiding the back-eddies which you can see forming on both sides as the current runs more swiftly in the center of the wave formation. Use caution, however, because some innocent-looking standing waves are actually piled-up water, obscuring your view of dangerous rocks. Always be sure before blindly passing along the crests of any standing waves downriver. A short distance below No. 10, watch for a large ponderosa pine tree on the left bank. It looks out of place when compared with the typical junipers which frequent this landscape. Also, you can see a classic example of massive columns of basalt on the right skyline's uppermost strata.*

11	7.9	1

IDENTIFICATION: River narrows. Standing waves midstream.

HOW TO: Pass through in center, on crests of standing waves, to avoid back-eddies.

12	8.1	1+

IDENTIFICATION: Big Island Riffle — Big Island splits the river about 100 yards downstream from No. 11. Take the right channel. Left channel is much shallower.

HOW TO: Position on right side of channel and pass along crests of whitewater. At the lower end of the island, move to within 10 feet of the right bank to avoid 2 large boulders which protrude out of the river bed and could cause upsets and damage.

COMMENTS: *Watch right bank to find a bench used by sightseers who like to watch river travellers in comfort! There is also a small camp located on the right bank at the head of the island.*

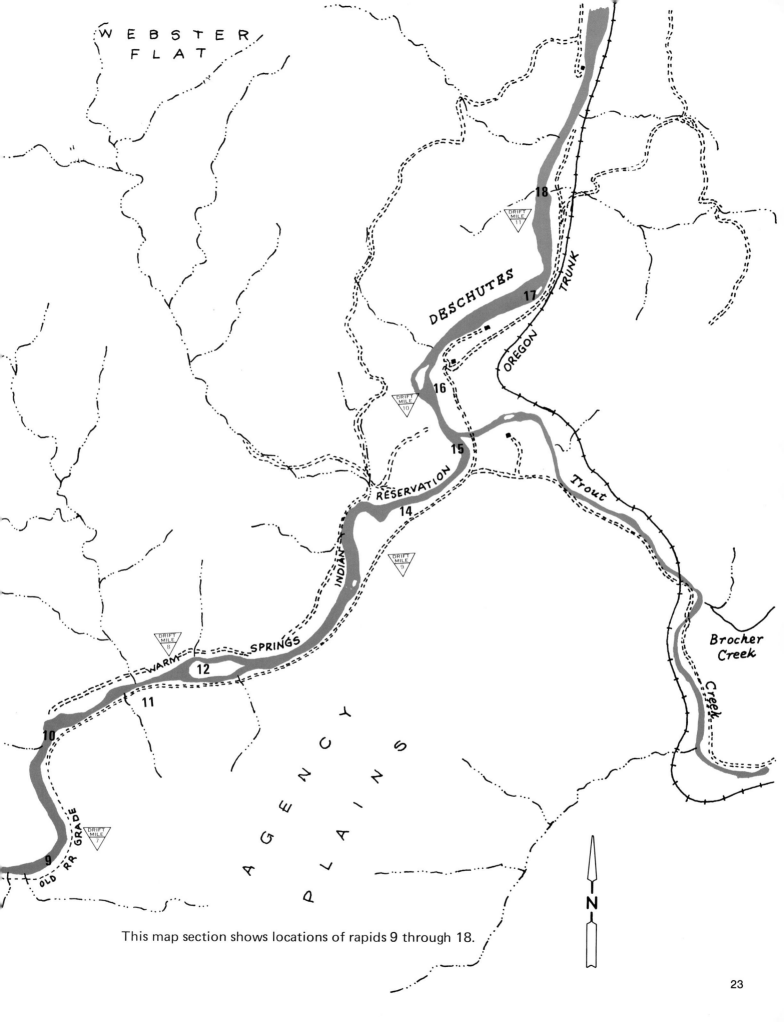

This map section shows locations of rapids 9 through 18.

*CHECKPOINT
NO. 1
9.0*

TROUT CREEK CAMPSITE — The 2,000 foot deep canyon widens. This is the only location on your entire float trip which is large enough to accomodate a townsite. Fortunately, due to its inaccessibility, none has ever been built. Toilets on the right bank mark the beginning of a large campsite which extends about a mile along the bank. A small island on the right side of the river also marks the beginning of this major campsite. Road access is available. A boat ramp permits launching and removing boats. Fishermen and river travelers use this campsite because of its facilities. Several hundred people can be accomodated. A good way to work off a big dinner is to take a hike to the top of the rimrock which overlooks Trout Creek flat. A great view of the entire Trout Creek area is possible. Look for scorpions under the rocks on the hillside.

Photo by Don Turcke

Hiker's view of Trout Creek Campsite.

24

14   9.3   1   IDENTIFICATION: Within 25 yards of the boat ramp of Trout Creek campsite, the river forms small standing waves in midstream.

HOW TO: Whitewater can be easily avoided or passed through in midstream.

COMMENTS: A short distance below No. 14, watch the right bank to find a brown 4x4 post with circular/triangular symbols. This is a bench marker which indicates the elevation of 1295 feet above sea level.

15   9.8   1+   IDENTIFICATION: Trout Creek enters on the right side. An abandoned black steel Oregon Trunk railroad bridge crosses the creek.

HOW TO: In high water, enter down the center of the calm slick on the right 1/3 of the river. Bedrock causes shallows in midstream. In low water, move tight against the left bank and pass through.

COMMENTS: Across the river, Columbia River basalt caps the John Day formation. Trout Creek is interesting because it marks the first view we have had of the present-day railroad operations (the Oregon Trunk). At this point the railway leaves the Deschutes River canyon and heads eastward to pass through the small community of Gateway, on its way to high Oregon plateaus. Many prehistoric fossils have been found in the canyon formed by Trout Creek. The headwaters of Trout Creek were located in the territory controlled by a rebellious Indian chief of the Walapi tribe of the Snake Indians. Paulina was his name. Paulina and his warriors often raided the Warm Springs Indian Reservation, stealing food, horses and cattle. His indiscriminate killing of whites and Indians alike caused him to be feared and hated. Some referred to him as "Atilla of the Sagelands." In one incident, Chief Poust-am-i-nie (of a peaceful group of Warm Springs Indians) was ambushed as his small hunting party passed through Trout Creek canyon. Paulina was responsible. 70 enraged Warm Springs Indians sought and received permission to leave the reservation to join the U.S. Army at The Dalles recruiting base. They wanted to join in the military's hunt for Paulina. In the 12 years between 1855 and 1867, reservation Indians worked in harmony with whites to try. to control the destruction and lawlessness of Paulina's band of rebels. But Paulina's time was running out. In the spring of 1867, Paulina and his braves stole a herd of cattle from an eastern Oregon ranch owned by Andrew Clarno. Four local ranchers, including Howard Maupin (who had been robbed several times by Paulina) tracked the rustled herd across the sagebrush prairie to the present-day site of Paulina Cove, near the headwaters of Trout Creek. The ranchers ambushed the Indians in the early dawn, as the Indians feasted on a breakfast of stolen beef. Two bullets from Howard Maupin's powerful Henry rifle brought Paulina's reign of terror to an end. Paulina's bones bleached in the sun where he fell. His scalp was nailed over Howard Maupin's doorway and was burned when a fire destroyed the building in 1902. Maupin and his family have been buried in a small pioneer graveyard along the edge of Trout Creek.

Rapid No.	Mileage	Class
16	10.0	2+

IDENTIFICATION: TROUT CREEK RAPIDS — This is the first rapids of any consequence. The river drops seven feet in the next two hundred yards. An island splits the river; Trout Creek flat is on the right bank. Take the right channel.

HOW TO: Move to the right channel. Watch for boulders midstream. Make your approach in dead center of the channel. Pass slightly to the right of the midstream boulder and, once into the current, pass straight through while pulling to the right to avoid turbulence created by large boulders. Do not get too close to the right bank because wooden beams protrude from it, and may cause damage.

COMMENTS: The upper end of the island is in Jefferson County, the lower end is in Wasco County. This arid area is dependent upon the river for irrigation. An old engine pumping device can be seen on the right bank as you pass through the rapids. The canyon will remain open for approximately 8 more miles. Today's Oregon Trunk railroad can be seen on the right bank as it follows the river downstream to the Columbia River.

Rafters head down Trout Creek rapids.

Dr. Jack Ingram stops to read this sign located at Trout Creek Campsite.

"FUTURE GENERATIONS WILL REMEMBER US FOR THE ROADS WE DON'T BUILD"

STEWART UDALL
SEC'Y OF INT.

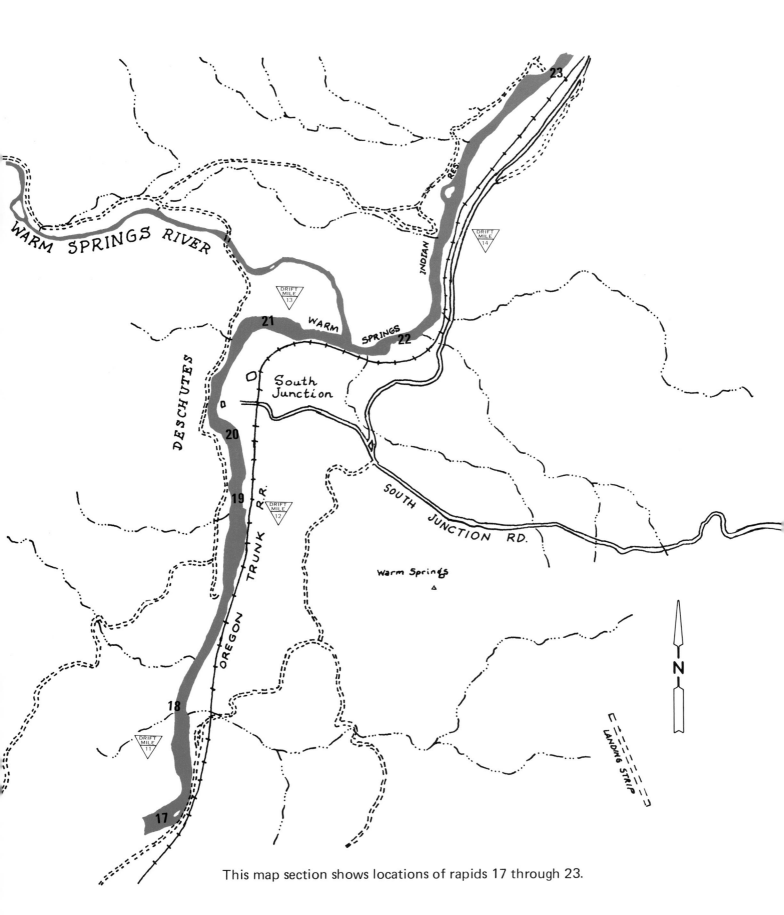

This map section shows locations of rapids 17 through 23.

Rapid No.	Mileage	Class
17	10.7	1+

IDENTIFICATION: A small island splits the river. The large flat of Trout Creek becomes smaller. Main channel to the left.

HOW TO: Stay in left channel. Avoid shallows in riverbed by maintaining your position in midchannel as you pass around a bend in the river.

—	11.0	—

COMMENTS: This area is known as "Redsides" or "Charley U'Rens Flat." The flat on the right bank was the site of a railroad construction camp in the years around 1910. This property was owned by Charley U'Rens and was a key camp in the battle of competing railroads as they raced their construction teams up the Deschutes canyon. U'Rens homesteaded this area between here and South Junction (a railroad station located about 1½ miles ahead). A chemical toilet is usually placed here by the Bureau of Land Management.

18	11.1	1

IDENTIFICATION: After passing to the right of a long, narrow island the river bends slightly to the left, forming minor standing waves.

HOW TO: No trouble. Pass down the center of the riffle.

19	12.0	1

IDENTIFICATION: A small midstream island splits the river. The large flat at South Junction begins on the right side. Main channel is left.

HOW TO: Avoid shallowing and rocks extending from the left bank. Stay in approximate midstream of left channel.

COMMENTS: Ahead, approximately 250 yards on the right bank, you can see the private summer residence of the owners of Green Valley Farms. The railroad station of South Junction is located several hundred yards from the river's edge. When the two railroads were being built up the Deschutes canyon (the Deschutes Railroad was supposed to pass along the east side of the river, the Oregon Trunk was to pass along the west side) it was found necessary for both to share a single track for a distance of 12 miles from this point. This led to a number of confrontations between the rival railroad crews. One example occurred when a small rockslide injured several Oregon Trunk workmen. They presumed the slide was caused by the Harriman crew. The Hill forces immediately sent up several armed guards to protect their workmen below the cliff. Harriman's crew, seeing the armed guards, reacted by immediately sending an equal number of armed men to patrol the adjacent plateau. Both crews remained jumpy for several days, but nobody was injured. The 12 mile stretch extended from the station at the north end (called North Junction) to this station (at the south end) called South Junction. In 1923, the Oregon Trunk Railroad abandoned its trackage from this point upriver, and shared running rights with the Deschutes Railroad trackage which exits from the Deschutes canyon via Trout Creek. Recently, South Junction has been the site of a fine purebred whiteface beef ranch and a China Pheasant rearing farm.

20	12.3	1+

IDENTIFICATION: In front of South Junction the river bends to the left, forming small standing waves.

HOW TO: Pass around bend by remaining approximately 1/3 off the left bank, thereby avoiding shallows along the right side of the river.

Fly fisherman, Gary Ingram, stops to admire his catch before releasing the Rainbow Trout.

Rapid No.	Mileage	Class
21	12.9	1+

IDENTIFICATION: At the lower end of South Junction Flat the river bends to the right, forming small standing waves.

HOW TO: Pass through in midstream, avoiding minor obstructions. As the river turns back to the left at the bottom of the riffle, exit from the whitewater on the crests of medium standing waves.

CHECKPOINT NO. 2
13.2

WARM SPRINGS RIVER ENTERS ON LEFT — Although the waters of the Warm Springs River are cool, it is named after the hot springs which exist upstream, near the Kah-Nee-Tah Resort. In 1859, General William Harney sent a military expedition through this area to search out a route to Salt Lake City, Utah. The expedition forded the Deschutes River on pontoon bridges at this site. The railroad is so well constructed that only one site washed out during the famous 1964 flood. The washout occurred when the Deschutes crested and fell, but the Warm Springs River continued to rise. The flow of the Warm Springs River shot across the surface of the Deschutes, passing directly into the east bank of the Deschutes, and washing out part of the bed of the railroad tracks and an old pumping station which used to supply water to steam locomotives. The rusty pipes are still visible protruding from the original concrete foundation at the water's edge.

22	13.4	1+

IDENTIFICATION: River shallows on the right side and makes an S-turn.

HOW TO: Stay within 20 feet of the left bank for easy passage.

23	14.8	1

IDENTIFICATION: Jersey Wye Riffle. A farmland flat on the right bank comes to an end. Road cuts can also be seen on the right bank. River shallows and bends to the right.

HOW TO: Pass through on right 1/3 of river to avoid shallows on left.

COMMENTS: Jersey Wye — This was the name of a turning station which used to be located on the flat on the east bank. The station was used by helper engines that steamed in from Metolius to assist southbound freight trains as they labored out of the canyon to the surrounding elevated plains. This is now a popular put-in site for rafters — they must carry their gear over the railroad tracks to reach the river. It is also your last chance to pull-out if you wish to avoid Whitehorse Rapids ahead. Tan colored rock cliffs on the west bank are part of the John Day geological formation. They are capped with a layer of darker basalt.

24	15.3	1

IDENTIFICATION: River bends to the left and forms small standing waves.

HOW TO: No trouble if you remain in midstream.

25	15.4	1

IDENTIFICATION: Approximately 150 yards downstream from No. 24. The buildings of Axford can be seen on the right bank.

HOW TO: Position yourself 1/3 off left bank and pass through with little trouble.

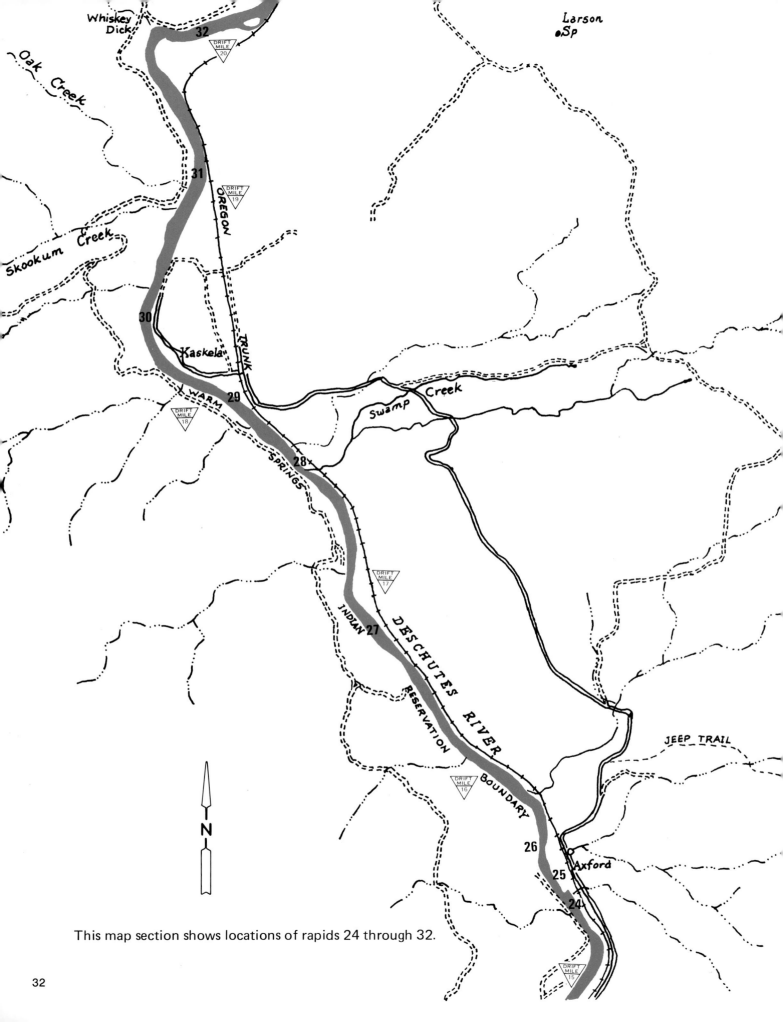

This map section shows locations of rapids 24 through 32.

32

26   15.6   1   IDENTIFICATION: A white house at Axford is on the right bank.

HOW TO: Position midstream and pass through with no trouble.

COMMENTS: The pioneer Axford family homesteaded this area. In the early '40's, when J.C. Meyers was track inspector for the Oregon Trunk Railroad company, the Axfords operated a small scale dude ranch. They had 3 or 4 guest cabins and saddle horses were available. It was an Axford who first discovered the vein of perlite in 1945 (you will come to the perlite mine at Dant, downstream).

27.   16.8   1+   IDENTIFICATION: River narrows and moves to left. Whitewater can be seen and heard. River shallows on right.

HOW TO: Position in midstream or slightly left of midstream. Move to left 1/3 of river as you pass through the riffle, to avoid large midstream boulders which form largest standing waves of the riffle. Maintain position about 1/3 off left bank as you pass out of the whitewater.

COMMENTS: A campground is located on the right bank. Toilets and a large flat area are available. No water. In early days, an old wing dam was constructed at this site to supply irrigation for this flat.

28   17.6   1+   IDENTIFICATION: River bends to left, shallowing on right side causing whitewater there. Kaskela can be seen about 3/4 mile ahead. A dry creek bed (Swamp Creek) enters on left bank.

HOW TO: Pass through in midriver, avoiding shallows on right side.

29   18.0   2   IDENTIFICATION: Kaskela Flat begins on right bank. River narrows and forms small standing waves all across its surface. Buildings of Kaskela are about 1/10 mile ahead.

HOW TO: Position about 1/3 off right bank. As river narrows, move to midstream to avoid submerged boulders on right 1/4 of river. Pass out on crests of standing waves.

—   18.1   —   *COMMENTS: The station of Kaskela is located on the right bank. Today, only summer residents live here. Malcolm A. Moody suggested the name for this town. Moody, a pioneer from The Dalles, was a U.S. Representative in Congress. The name "Kaskela" was that of the first Warm Springs Indian chief after the establishment of the agency. At one time an old steam shovel was displayed on the flat between the river and the railroad tracks. Its purpose was to construct a sawmill at this site. The logs were to be of pine, possibly cut on the Warm Springs reservation and floated down the Deschutes to the mill. The finished product was to go out over the Oregon Trunk railroad. The plan never materialized. Kaskela lies at the foot of the Mutton Mountain Range, which you will pass through as you continue your journey downstream. The Mutton Mountains were named for the large numbers of wild mountain sheep which originally lived in this area. This species is known as "Rimrock" or "lava Bed" sheep. They no longer inhabit the slopes. Peter Skene Ogden made reference to the wild sheep in his reports of 1825. Biologists believe the wild sheep could not withstand the diseases introduced by domestic sheep when settlers moved into this area.*

30 18.4 1+ IDENTIFICATION: River bends to the right, small whitewater standing waves are formed. River shallows on right and boulders can be seen causing standing waves. This riffle is located in the approximate middle of Kaskela Flat.

HOW TO: **Position in midriver and pass through with no trouble.**

31 19.1 1+ IDENTIFICATION: Green colored rock on left bank marks beginning of this gentle riffle. Water holds riffle formation for about 8/10 mile, around bend in river. On left bank several small buildings can be seen.

HOW TO: **Pass through the first part in midriver, then move to the right side of the river to avoid shallows and midriver boulders. Finally, move back to midriver to avoid protruding shallows from the right bank. At the very end of the riffle, a midriver boulder must be avoided by passing slightly to the left of it.**

COMMENTS: There is a small campsite on the right bank, approximately 100 yards before the final boulder. Ahead, on the right bank, a large flat marks the site of gravel deposits used by railroad construction crews during the early days of the railroad. Also, interesting ribs and pinnacles have been eroded from the rock structure of the canyon walls ahead.

32 19.9 1 IDENTIFICATION: Whiskey Dick Riffle — River narrows, water passes to the left side of the river as the river bends to the right.

HOW TO: **Position yourself 1/3 off the right bank and pass through with no trouble.**

COMMENTS: Campsite on right bank.

Two men on horseback ford the Deschutes River in the summer of 1909. Note railroad construction grade in background.

Courtesy of Mrs. H.E. Carleton

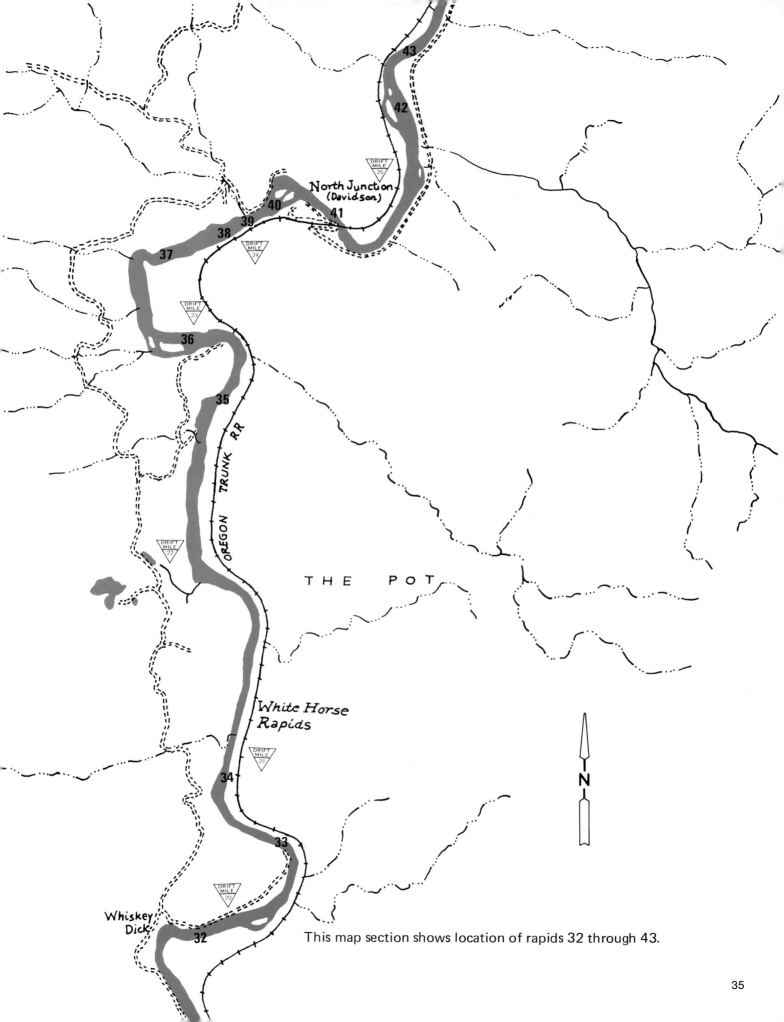

43

42

DRIFT MILE 25

North Junction
(Davidson)

40

39

41

38

37

DRIFT MILE 24

DRIFT MILE 23

36

35

OREGON TRUNK RR

DRIFT MILE 22

THE POT

White Horse
Rapids

DRIFT MILE 21

34

33

DRIFT MILE 20

Whiskey
Dick

32

This map section shows location of rapids 32 through 43.

N

Rapid No.	Mileage	Class	
33	20.6	2+	**IDENTIFICATION: WARNING SHELF FOR WHITEHORSE** — Cliffs on right side of river show signs of being subject to extreme pressures during volcanic formation. Green lichen colors sunshine-exposed surfaces. A shelf of this resistant rock stretches across the riverbed to form the rapids.

HOW TO: Enter by positioning 20 feet off the left bank. Enter V-slick, then pull back across the river (to the right) to miss boulders both on left and in midstream.

COMMENTS: This is the last piece of whitewater before Whitehorse Rapids ahead.

Rapid No.	Mileage	Class	
34	20.8	4	*****SCOUTING MANDATORY***SCOUT FROM RIGHT BANK*****

WHITEHORSE RAPIDS — *In the first 21 miles, since your put-in at Warm Springs, the river has descended 190 feet. This rate is comparable to that of the Colorado River in the Grand Canyon. Immediately ahead, the river will drop 75 feet in the next 3 miles. In fact, the main part of Whitehorse Rapids will drop 25 feet in the first 300 yards! Although difficult, it is possible to line a boat through these rapids along the left bank. In 1834, Nathaniel Wyeth (a fur-trader in these parts) reported that Whitehorse Rapids would present no trouble for a competent boatman. In 1923, a party of 3 surveyors came downriver without difficulty, but they capsized at this point. Of the 3, only 1 man survived by spending the night clinging to a midstream boulder at the lower end of the rapids. He was rescued the next day. Every year there are near-tragedies at this rapids, so proceed with caution. Drownings have averaged 6 per year along the Deschutes River, and Whitehorse claims its share. Notice that the rapids have been formed because the river has cut its way through the Mutton Mountain rock structure, which is unstable in this area. Frequent rockslides plague the railroad as it passes this point. You can see a fence that activates the block signals on each end of the sheer rock wall next to the railroad tracks. This fence will work to warn engineers when rocks or slides stretch its spring-loaded wires. Once stretched, electrical contacts are made and the block signals' warning lights are activated.*

IDENTIFICATION: Within 100 yards of No. 33, watch the right bank to find the electrified fence which the railroad uses as a warning device. Also, the river current slows and there is a stretch of the right bank which can be used as a docking space so that you can get out to scout the rapids. Don't go too far, or you will be into the rapids before you are ready for them! Stay close to the right bank to avoid problems. Rattlesnakes and poison oak frequent this area, so be careful. To scout, climb up to the railroad tracks on the right bank and walk down them until you can get a good view of the rapids. The whitewater extends about 2 miles, so you probably won't want to walk its entire length. The most difficult part is at the beginning of the rapids, and you will find a flat area overlooking this section within a short distance of your boat. The most complicated maneuvering is in the first 200 yards, but you must remain alert to avoid numerous large midstream boulders for the remainder of this 2-mile rapids. Some choose an alternate passage along the left bank at Stage One.

IDENTIFICATION: There are three ways to run Whitehorse rapids. At high river flows the safest route is about 30 feet off the right bank. During low flows the easiest passage is found along the left bank. The center run is passable at most flows and is the most challenging. How to: Stage I.

HOW TO: Right Run: Enter the rapid 30 feet off the right bank and pass directly over the first white water break on the slick. Maintain position passing 15 feet to the left of a large round boulder 50 feet below. Extreme care must be taken not to allow the current to force you into the rock boulders along the right bank.

IDENTIFICATION: Left Run: Identify the island located about 50 feet from the left bank. Directly above the island there are grass tuffs and willows growing from exposed bedrock creating the impression of a "false island." There is a shelf of bedrock that joins the bottom of the false island to the upper rocks of the main island.

HOW TO: Position as close to the right side of the "false island" as possible, passing within six feet to the right of a low flat boulder protruding into the river from the island. Once past this obstruction pull to within 8 feet of the upper island and maintain position until dropping over a rock shelf with a three foot vertical drop. Once over the drop, position within 8 feet to the left of the main island to avoid large standing waves 15 feet from the left bank of the island. Once past the island ride the crests of the large standing waves in midstream. Center run (Stage I): as in book. Stage I.

Whitehorse tricked this cowboy right out of his boat.

Aerial view of Whitehorse Rapids as it cuts its path through the Mutton Mountains.

CENTER RUN: HOW TO: STAGE ONE — Identify boulder "A" about 50 feet off right bank, midway between right bank and shallows in middle of river. Also, identify boulder "B" about 20 feet downstream from "A" and about 35 feet off the right bank. An entry V-slick forms between these 2 boulders. Enter this slick about 3 feet on the right side of "A," passing between "A" and "B" by pulling to the right (thereby passing within 3 feet of the left side of "B"). Once past "B" immediately pull hard to the right to avoid boulder "C," which is another 50 feet downstream from "B." (Notice that "A" and "C" are in line with each other in midcurrent, and that "B" is slightly to their right. However, because of the pattern of the current, your boat will be forced into "C" by the merging of the water flows. The net effect is to force your boat directly into boulder "C." Boulder "C" is positioned just a few feet upstream from the head of a small midstream island (covered with small willows and grass). Once past "C" look ahead to avoid a large turbulence on the right side of the river, near the end of the island. From here on, avoid midstream boulders as necessary. Near the end of Stage One, identify 3 large midriver boulders which could cause trouble. Pass close to the right bank if you wish to avoid them altogether. Now the water calms as you pass out of Stage One, and you have a short distance to prepare for Stage Two.

Rapid
No. Mileage Class

—   21.5   —   **HOW TO: STAGE TWO** — At the end of the straight stretch of the river, it bends to the left and Whitehorse Rapids continues. Set-up in the midriver V-slick and avoid the large standing waves on both sides. Continue through the second stage on the crests of the large standing waves in midriver, for about 100 yards. When the water calms once again you have completed Stage Two, and you have a short distance to prepare for Stage Three.

—   21.8   —   **HOW TO: STAGE THREE** — After about 100 yards of calm water, the river bends to the right. Large boulders stand high and dry in midriver. Shallows form across the river's width. Identify 3 large boulders extending from left bank to midriver. You must position within 40 feet of left bank. The right channel is impassable. Pass within 4 feet on the left side of the far left boulder. Once past this boulder, pull back across the river to avoid dangerous obstacles on left. Pass within 6 feet of midriver rock island with bushes growing on it, and position in midriver for the remainder of the rapids. Maneuver to the right or left as necessary from your midriver position. These maneuvers can be accomplished safely if you keep working room and look ahead constantly. Also, avoid large standing waves (which may hide boulders and treacherous suckholes).

COMMENTS: Whitehorse Rapids was a 2-mile adventure. At the end of Stage Three you will find a campsite on the right bank. This is a good place to stop, repair damage, compare experiences and prepare for the next part of your journey. If you wish to camp overnight, you will find toilet facilities and a large camping area. Across the river you will see a large rock pinnacle which has created a big back-eddy at its base. This back-eddy usually supplies campers with firewood. Remember, land on the west bank is reservation land and is private property. The 2-mile stretch of whitewater behind you is considered to be the best fishing stretch on the lower 97 miles of the Deschutes River. In earlier times this campground site was used by railroad construction crews. Old road beds and pits for the storage of blasting powder are still visible. Water hemlock is a notorious poisonous plant. It grows in this area and has caused deaths along the river as unknowing travellers have mistaken its leaves and roots for other edible plants, such as wild celery, wild parsnip, etc. Many campers like to walk the railroad tracks to the railroad tunnel which is visible from the campgrounds. Be careful, it is possible to be trapped in the tunnel! The brightly colored sediments of the bluffs to the east are tilted up on edge. There is intense folding of these rock strata of the Clarne Formation of Eocene Time (dating back some 50-70 million years).

The boatman is positioning the drift boat just to the right of boulder "A." The sub-zero temperatures in January made it necessary for the author to wear a protective face mask).

Notice how the boat rides the V-slick to the right of boulder "A." Boulder "B" can be identified just to the right of the boatman's oar.

"OOPS." This is boulder "C" which is referred to in the "How To." Obviously, navigator Tony Offutt did not read the "How To" section very carefully.

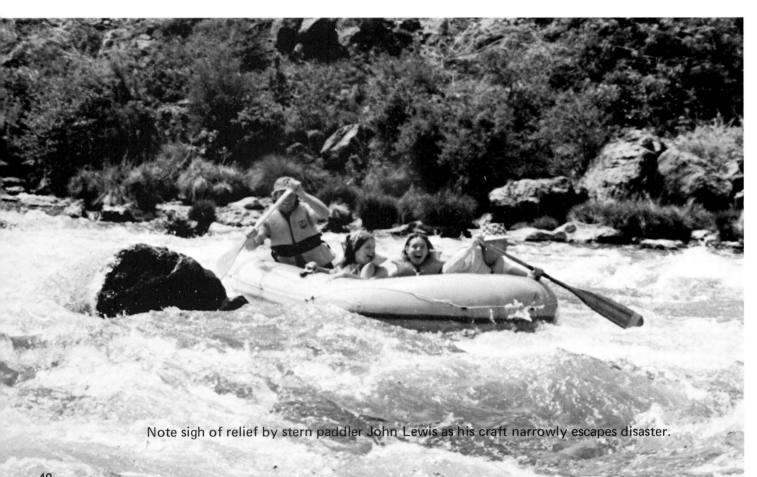

Note sigh of relief by stern paddler John Lewis as his craft narrowly escapes disaster.

Running Whitehorse on the right.

Mike McLucas running Whitehorse.

Rapid No.	Mileage	Class	

35   22.7   1   IDENTIFICATION: Approximately 100 yards below the large campground at the foot of Whitehorse Rapids.

HOW TO: Pass through this minor whitewater in midstream.

COMMENTS: Tortured basalt reveals the volcanic origins of the rock forming the Mutton Mountains.

36   23.0   2   IDENTIFICATION: 3 railroad shacks on large flat on right. Island splits river, main channel to right.

HOW TO: Take right channel. Position yourself about midstream to avoid the shallows on the right side, and pass through on small standing waves.

37   23.7   1+   IDENTIFICATION: About 100 yards below the end of No. 36. River bends to the right and shallows on right riverbed.

HOW TO: Position in midriver for the first 50 yards, then move to within 20 feet of the left bank to avoid severe shoals on the right.

COMMENTS: Davidson Flat campsite on the right bank can be reached by pulling back immediately after the shoals are passed. Toilet. Can suit large party. The steep cliff wall across the river (on the west bank) was considered impassable by the rail- roads.

38   23.9   1   IDENTIFICATION: Small standing waves arise ahead.

HOW TO: Pass down center with no trouble.

Aerial view of railroad crossing the Deschutes River at North Junction.

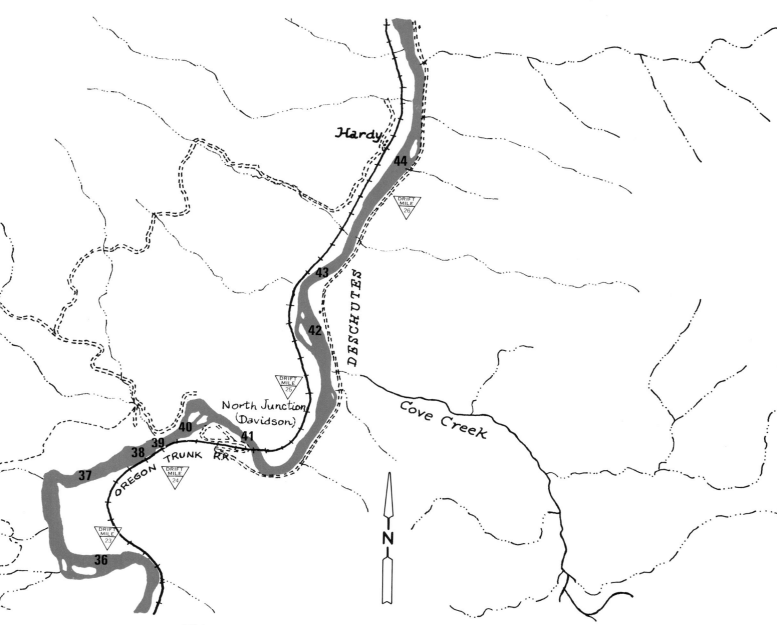

This map section shows the locations of rapids 36 through 44.

Rapid No.	Mileage	Class	
39	24.0	1+	IDENTIFICATION: River narrows as rocks extend into river from right bank. **HOW TO: Position yourself in midriver and pass through.**
40	24.2	1+	IDENTIFICATION: North Junction houses can be seen on right side at this riffle's entrance. River splits in 3 parts because of 2 midstream islands. Main channel is left channel. **HOW TO: Position about 1/3 off left bank. Avoid back-eddy on left side and continue past island.**

NORTH JUNCTION RAILROAD BRIDGE CROSSES RIVER — *North Junction was established in 1910. The present-day name for it is "Davidson." It was named "North Junction" because it marked the northern junction of the two railroads which competed for development of the Deschutes River canyon. The southern junction is 12 miles away, and is called "South Junction." The history of this area is exciting because it involved battles for right-of-way between the two railroad lines and their owners, railroad barons James Hill and Edward Harriman. At this place, in 1910, the battles reached their climax. Harriman's chief construction engineer Boschke received a false telegram from the Hill group, urgently demanding his return to Galveston, Texas to repair damage to the Galveston seawall (which Boschke had recently completed), but Boschke said he knew that he had built the seawall to stand and nothing could destroy it, so he ignored the fake telegram. Armed guards were posted by both battling crews, and when local landowner Frank Smith found himself embroiled in the railroad war's right-of-way conflict, the Federal Government found it necessary to intervene. The result was enforcement of the Federal "Canyon Act" which pressured Hill and Harriman to agree to joint usage of a single track between here and South Junction. After both railroads had been in operation for a number of years, it was realized that Bend could not support two independent railroads. New railroad management decided to consolidate the best parts of both trackages. Because of the heavier-duty construction of the Oregon Trunk trackage, it was the trackage of choice between this point and the Columbia River. The Oregon Trunk grade was more consistent than the Union Pacific grade. Over 9,000,000 cubic yards of solid rock was moved by pick, shovel and wheelbarrow when the grade was cut into the canyon walls. Several years ago, a train derailment occurred here, tearing the bridge apart and tying up the canyon for almost six weeks.*

Rapid No.	Mileage	Class	
41	24.5	1	IDENTIFICATION: Railroad bridge crosses river.

HOW TO: Pass to right or left of midriver stanchion of bridge. No trouble.

—	25.1	—	

COMMENTS: A campsite is located on the right bank about 50 yards below a small island. The small island on the right bank marks the beginning of the Deschutes Club. The club was founded in the early 1930's by a group of dedicated fishermen.

42	25.3	1+	IDENTIFICATION: Island splits river. Main channel to right.

HOW TO: Take right channel. Position about 1/3 off island (island is to your left). Then move to midchannel to avoid small island at lower end of whitewater.

COMMENTS: Two ranchers named Hinton and Ward operated a sheep camp on the flat extending along the river for several hundred yards on the right bank. One story says their sheepherders used to throw haywire into the river along this stretch and fishermen were bothered enough by their lines being tangled in the wire to name this stretch "Wire Hole." Another story says the hole was named after Frank B. Wire, one of the founding members of the Deschutes Club, who was a fly-tier, fisherman and craftsman of one-piece split-bamboo rods.

43	25.6	1+	IDENTIFICATION: River bends to right, leading into No. 43.

HOW TO: Position in midstream and pass through on crests of small standing waves.

A summer steelhead about to be landed.

44 26.3 1 IDENTIFICATION: The buildings of Hardy railroad station are on the left bank. Hardy was a traveling freight agent for the Oregon Trunk for many years. A small island is located on the right side of the river. This station was also called Nathan for a number of years.

HOW TO: River shallows. Pass through in midstream.

COMMENTS: The old railroad's water tower concrete piers can still be seen. They are surrounded by poplar trees.

45 26.8 1+ IDENTIFICATION: Island splits river. Main channel to right.

HOW TO: Position yourself in right channel in midstream. Avoid shallows and midstream rock at lower end of island. Pass by second smaller island in midstream, also.

COMMENTS: Just upstream from No. 45 is "Rattlesnake Hole." Berkley Snow's History of the Deschutes Club *relates a humorous incident experienced by Naomi Epping and her dog, Bokko. They were fishing one day, years ago, and Naomi hooked a fighting steelhead. Suddenly, a rattlesnake buzzed, Bokko barked, the steelhead jumped and the line snapped. And Naomi sat down in the river!*

46 27.0 1 IDENTIFICATION: A small house is located on the flat on the right bank. This is referred to as Red Birch Camp on Green's Flat.

HOW TO: Stay midriver and pass through.

COMMENTS: There is a small hot springs on the left bank that used to be an Indian bathing site. They would soak in the hot water until their bodies were heated, then they jumped into the river for the invigorating effect. In the early 1940's, the local Japanese converted the hot springs into a bathhouse with a wooden tub for their daily baths. A grass fire burned the original structure and only its foundation can be located by careful searching.

47 27.2 1+ IDENTIFICATION: Small island splits river.

HOW TO: Take left channel. Stay positioned in midchannel and pass through.

48 27.6 1+ IDENTIFICATION: House on the right (known as "Hernando's Hideaway"). River splits — take left channel.

HOW TO: Take left channel. Position midstream and pass through. Once through, pass to right or left of Dill Island, which has a dramatic rock pillar at its head.

COMMENTS: Note the old Deschutes Railroad tunnel Number 5, on the right bank. This tunnel is presently used by cars as they make their way upriver on the road. The road is private and is not open to the public. Dill Island was named after an early-day fishing guide, Don Dill.

49 27.8 1 IDENTIFICATION: Minor whitewater forms on both sides of island.

HOW TO: Proceed down midchannel.

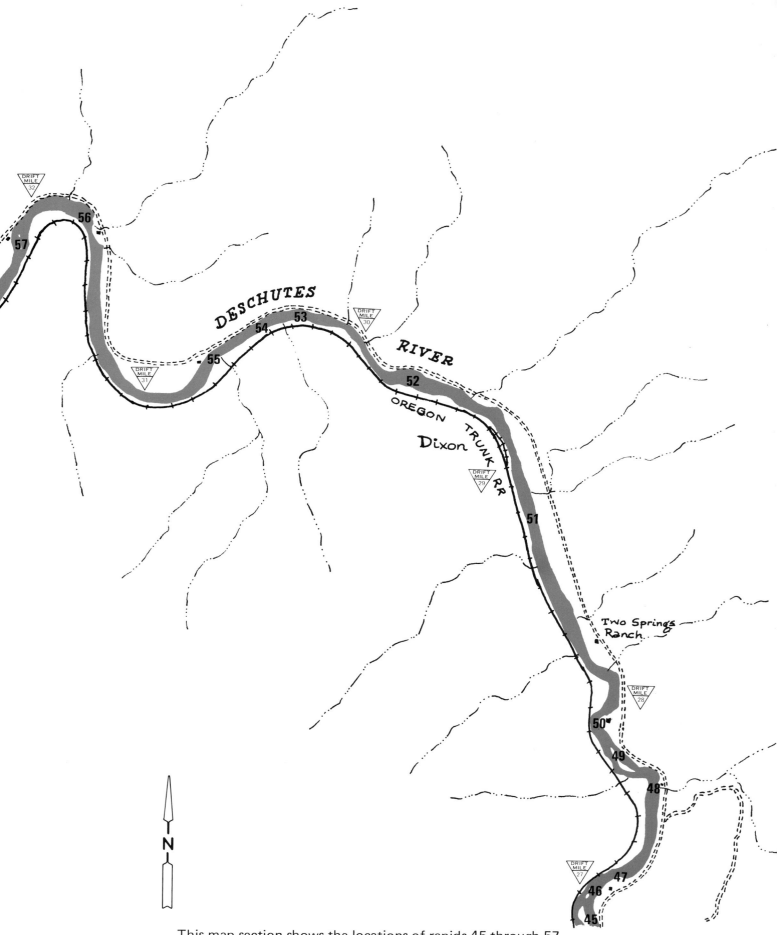

This map section shows the locations of rapids 45 through 57.

COMMENTS: The cabin on the flat on the right bank is known as "Chateau Rim-rock." It was named after the castle-like monolith rising from the river's edge across from it.

Rapid No.	Mileage	Class
50	27.9	1

IDENTIFICATION: Rimrock Riffle. River crosses to right side, forming riffle on right.

HOW TO: Remain with the current and pull off the right bank.

—	28.2	—

COMMENTS: The power boat "Deadline" sign on the right bank gives notice to power boat operators that further progress upstream is forbidden. This site also marks the end of the Warm Springs Indian Reservation on the left bank. The reservation boundary extends to midriver. The flat on the right bank extends for about 1 mile, and is known as the Hinton and Ward Hay Ranch. Two Springs Ranch is located at the upstream end of the flat.

51	28.8	1

IDENTIFICATION: John's Ruffles. Approximately 3/4 mile stretch of smooth water changes when river surface develops a minor chop.

HOW TO: Proceed down center.

COMMENTS: John Legar operated the hay ranch for Hinton and Ward years ago. To John, an avid fisherman, all riffling waters were "ruffles." Therefore, it only seemed good sense to his friends to designate this stretch of the river as "John's Ruffles."

—	29.2	—

COMMENTS: As the river bends gently to the left you enter "Rainbow Bend," named after the fish that populate this stretch. The railroad station named "Dixon" is on the left bank. A power cable can be seen above the river.

52	29.7	2

IDENTIFICATION: A small shack can be seen on the right bank. Dixon is approximately 1/4 mile behind, on the left bank. River bends to the right. Water flows to the left side, forming standing waves.

HOW TO: Enter in midriver and ride the standing waves for about 75 yards.

53	30.2	1+

IDENTIFICATION: Approximately 200 yards after No. 52. River bends to left.

HOW TO: Move to right 1/3 of river and maintain position about 30 feet off right bank around curve.

54	30.4	1

IDENTIFICATION: River surface forms small chop across width.

HOW TO: Remain midstream and pass through.

COMMENTS: A dramatic erosive action on the right has formed caves, natural bridges and pillars.

55	30.7	1+

IDENTIFICATION: Building on right side at beginning of riffle. The benchmark on the right bank is for an elevation of 1026 feet above sea level.

HOW TO: Position in midriver and hold position as you are carried around the bend in the river.

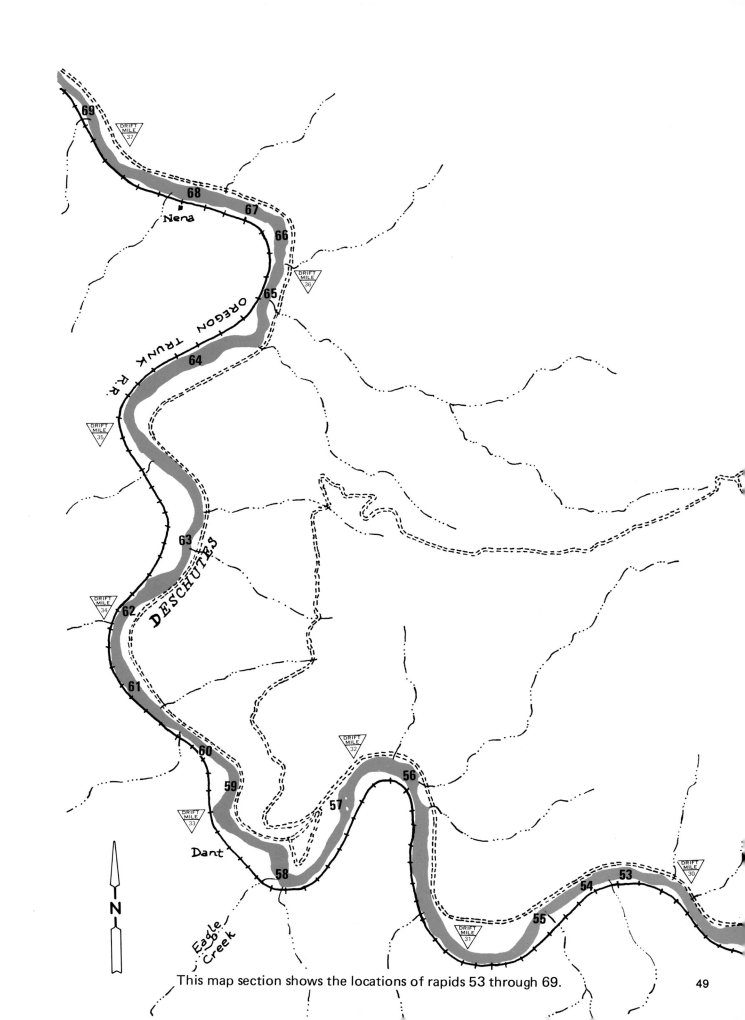

This map section shows the locations of rapids 53 through 69.

COMMENTS: *The flat on the right bank is known as "Buck Pasture." As you continue downriver, watch the right bank to find a campsite suitable for a large group. Toilet. Water retention by the slopes in this area permits tree growth, whereas downstream the trees are almost nonexistent. Denser lavas hold moisture from the snowfall on the high elevations of the pinnacles and crags. At approximately mile 31.7 there is a large stillwater area on the right side of the river which is known as "Big Eddy" by local fishermen. Also, on the right side you can see another railroad tunnel. Some 300 yards upstream from the tunnel is an area known as "Rattlesnake Pit" because of the large numbers of rattlesnakes which used to be found here.*

56   31.8   1+   IDENTIFICATION: Tuma Bend. A house can be seen on the right bank. A beautiful rock face lies ahead. River turns to left.

HOW TO: River forms whitewater which is easily negotiated by positioning 1/3 off left bank, and holding position around bend in river.

57   32.1   1+   IDENTIFICATION: Island in midstream splits river. Take right channel. Flat on right bank.

HOW TO: Take right channel and ride through on standing waves.

58   32.6   1+   IDENTIFICATION: Perlite Riffle. The railroad station on the left bank was originally named Freida, but today is known as Dant. The large flat on the right bank is called "Clubhouse Flat."

HOW TO: Easily negotiated in midstream.

COMMENTS: *Clubhouse Flat is the location of the Deschutes Club's first clubhouse. Berkley Snow's* History of the Deschutes Club *relates the story of the 1937 business meeting, during which two over-involved fishermen became so absorbed in their trout-catching/releasing activities they had to be forcibly brought to the business meeting by the club's sergeant-at-arms. In 1945 a prospector named Axford discovered a type of volcanic glass (called "perlite") in the cliffs on both sides of the river at this site. The original developers of the area were Dant and Russell of Portland, who mined the perlite for use in plasterboard and acoustical tile. You can still see the Lady Frances mine on the west canyon wall, about 200 feet above river level. The perlite product was named "Dantore," and it was shipped downgrade to Portland. Originally, this station was named "Frieda" (after a wife of one of the railroad executives), but the name was changed to "Dant" when the mining operation was established. Electricity brought to the mine for its operation also permitted local homeowners to modernize and use electricity to power their irrigation pumps. A war surplus lifeboat, originally purchased by the mining operation, still serves as the ferry crossing to Dant from the east bank. The perlite mine is no longer active. The houses vacated in the aftermath of the perlite "boom" have since been purchased and are presently occupied by members of a sport fishermen's group, the Deschutes Homeowners Association. The gate on the right side of the river is called the "Iron Curtain" because it had a reputation of always being locked. The tunnel at Dant is the narrowest on this side of the river. In the '40's a mine-worker was trapped on foot in the tunnel. He was killed by a train. If you are ever in a similar predicament you can escape if you lie down flat on the floor of the tunnel, pressed against the wall, parallel to the track. Close your eyes, plug your ears, press against the wall, lie flat and wait until the entire train has passed before moving.*

61   33.8   2   IDENTIFICATION: Flat appears on right bank; small canyon opens on right.

HOW TO: Position midriver and ride through medium standing waves for the next 75 yards.

COMMENTS: Campsite located on the flat bar on the right.

62   34.0   2   IDENTIFICATION: Located at bottom of flat bar on right, about 200 yards below the end of No. 61. Identify rock in left center stream.

HOW TO: Position about 15 feet on right side of rock, in approximate midriver. Enter main V-slick to ride out an enjoyable series of standing waves.

63   34.4   1+   IDENTIFICATION: Island splits river; take either channel (but stay within 30 feet of the island).

HOW TO: Stay within 30 feet of the island, and once past the end of the island, move to midstream to avoid rocks in the right riverbed.

COMMENTS: A small campsite is located on the right bank, approximately 50 yards past the small house.

—   34.9   —   *COMMENTS: An old house is located on the flat on the left bank. In early times, sheep-shearing and lambing teams lived here as they took care of the large numbers of sheep raised on the mountainside. The wooden remains of the original ferry crossing (used to transport men and supplies across the river) can still be seen about 150 yards downstream from the house. Pastures and agricultural land area were cleared of rocks by building perimeter fences up the smooth canyon slopes on the west side.*

—   35.1   —   *COMMENTS: As the river bends to the right, a large flat can be seen on the right side. This is known as "Hunt's Hay Ranch." At the beginning of the flat, the stretch of water is called "Pumphouse Hole" (referring to the old pump which used to irrigate the ranch).*

64   35.5   1   IDENTIFICATION: River forms small standing waves as water moves from left to right side of river. Hunt's Hay Ranch on right flat. The dwelling you can see is the Deschutes Club's caretaker's residence.

HOW TO: Enter V-slick and ride out on crests of small waves. Downstream 50 yards, river shallows in center, so remain in right 1/3 of river until current carries you to midstream. Remain midstream for next 200 yards as current picks up speed slightly. Avoid large back-eddies on either side if you want to continue forward progress.

65   35.9   1   IDENTIFICATION: Mounds of gravel on right bank.

HOW TO: Move to left 1/3 of the river to enter V-slick, then ride out on crests of small standing waves.

66   36.1   1   IDENTIFICATION: Large crack in right canyon wall.

HOW TO: Position midriver and enter main V-slick. Ride out on crests of small standing waves.

67	36.3	1	IDENTIFICATION: Several caves are obvious.

HOW TO: Remain midriver.

COMMENTS: *Blasting the railroad grade exposed these tunnels. Lava tunnels are the result of rapid cooling of surface flow. The molten lava may continue to flow for a long time, but when the supply of fresh lava slows down at the source, there will not be enough coming through to fill the volume of the tunnel, causing an empty space at the top of the tunnel. Such lava tunnels are quite common, and prehistoric man in this area made good use of them.*

68	36.6	1	IDENTIFICATION: Island splits river in front of Nena station. Either channel is navigable, but the left channel is easier.

HOW TO: Take left channel midstream. Below island, the river current stiffens for several hundred yards. Remain midstream to avoid back-eddies on both sides.

COMMENTS: *A campsite is located below the island, approximately 100 yards on the right bank. "Nena" is an Indian word meaning "tall, white cottonwood trees." Years ago, when Willis Roberts was section foreman at Nena station on the west bank, he would drive his car to Maupin for supplies. Parking his car across the river, he would paddle his rubber boat to his home on the west bank. One evening he left his car and carried a bulky box of groceries cautiously down the dark riverbank to his waiting craft moored below. Suddenly, he realized he had stepped on a coiled rattlesnake in the darkness. Instinctively, he jumped out of the rattler's striking range, throwing his groceries all over the riverbank. He wasn't injured, so he crossed to his home and awaited morning's light to salvage his supplies.*

69	37.1	1	IDENTIFICATION: Just past the flat on the right bank (with campsite). River moves to right side.

HOW TO: Position in approximate midriver, ride safely and swiftly through.

—	38.1	—	COMMENTS: *A campsite with nice shade trees is located on the right bank as you pass a big bend in the river. No toilets or water.*

70	38.2	1	IDENTIFICATION: About 100 yards past the campsite on the right bank. A large boulder is on the left. The cattle gate on the right bank marks the beginning of the whitewater riffle and the end of the controlled access to the Deschutes Club.

HOW TO: Enter in midriver and current will carry you through on crests of small standing waves.

71	38.3	1	IDENTIFICATION: Approximately 300 yards below No. 70.

HOW TO: Remain midriver and pass through with no trouble.

COMMENTS: *Cliffs on right bank have thick columnar basalt columns on top layer. We are leaving the heart of the Mutton Mountains.*

72	38.5	1	IDENTIFICATION: Sign reading: "Entering Public Land" on the right; cliffs of brickbat basalt form hanging valleys and waterfalls.

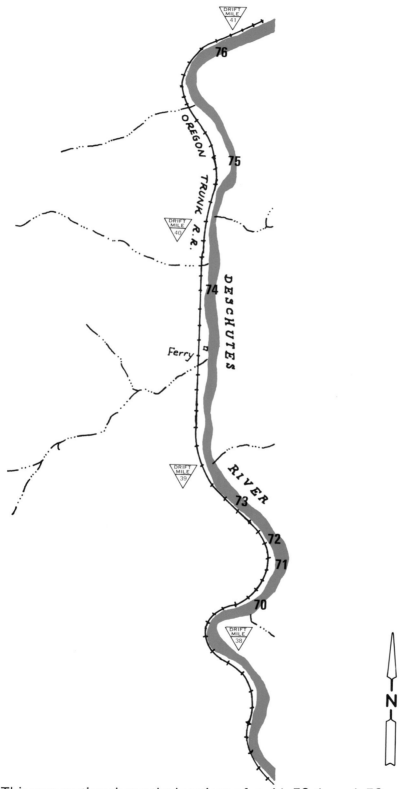

This map section shows the locations of rapids 70 through 76.

HOW TO: Enter in midriver and pass through with no problem.

COMMENTS: Engineers dangled by ropes along the east bank of the river as they surveyed their lines for the railbeds which were to pass through this section of the canyon.

73 38.9 1+   IDENTIFICATION: Rock outcropping in midriver.

HOW TO: Pass down either side, then return to midriver to ride out on small standing waves.

CHECKPOINT NO. 4 39.4   *NENA CREEK ENTERS ON LEFT SIDE — Nena Creek rises in the Mutton Mountains in the northwest corner of the Warm Springs Indian reservation. A campsite is located approximately 100 feet below the creek on the left bank. A natural pasture is about 1,000 feet above you on the plateau to the west. Years ago, there was a ferry crossing at this point, which transported livestock from the east bank to grazing lands up in the natural pasture.*

74 39.8 2   IDENTIFICATION: 300 yards below Nena Creek; shallows extend across width of river; Devil's Canyon can be seen opening downstream on east bank.

HOW TO: Position about 30 feet off left bank and enter V-slot. Ride out on crests of small standing waves. Water calms for short distance, then river narrows noticeably at the lower end of the rapids. Navigate this second stage in midriver.

75 40.3 1   IDENTIFICATION: Approximately 200 yards below end of No. 74; river bends sharply to the left.

HOW TO: Remain midstream.

— 40.8 —   *COMMENTS: Campsite on right bank. If you wish to avoid running two major rapids ahead, you may choose to pull out at either this or one of the next three campsites, within the next mile and a half.*

76 40.9 1   IDENTIFICATION: Located 200 yards below campsite on right bank; railroad markers can be seen on left bank.

HOW TO: Remain midstream. No trouble.

77 41.1 1   IDENTIFICATION: Midstream boulder causes minor whitewater.

HOW TO: Pass one either side of boulder.

COMMENT: Campsite on right bank, approximately 50 yards below No. 77. Toilet.

78 41.2 1   IDENTIFICATION: Minor whitewater forms; small boulder on left riverbed protrudes.

HOW TO: Remain in midriver and pass easily.

79 41.4 1   IDENTIFICATION: Small standing waves flow over boulder about 25 feet off left bank.

"boulder suckhole" and its powerful hydraulics, which can tip even the largest rafts. This "boulder suckhole" is probably the most dangerous single obstacle on the river (other than Sherar's Falls). Once past this obstacle, remain in the right 1/3 of the river to avoid 2 downstream midriver boulders. Within 50 yards you will enter calmer waters. A back-eddy on the right bank is conveniently located, should you wish to bail-out your boat or wait for other members of your party.

Photo by Don Turcke

Even flipping a raft in Boxcar could not dampen the enthusiasm of these river runners.

COMMENTS: *Boxcar Rapids is known by several names. It has also been called "Lower Wapinitia Rapids" and "Train Hole Rapids." Local residents refer to it as "the waterfall two miles upriver." One of the worst accidents in the history of the Oregon Trunk occurred at this site in March, 1954. Boxcar Rapids gets its name from this tragedy. Engineer Ernie Barton and Fireman Earl Sutton were at the controls of lead engine No. 857 as it rounded the curve on the west side of the river. The down-river track was blocked by a rockslide and they couldn't stop in time. The three diesel-electric locomotives and a dozen boxcars were derailed. They jumped the tracks and wedged themselves into the narrow cut. One boxcar and the lead loco-motive, which carried Barton and Sutton, plunged into the swollen Deschutes, dis-appearing completely. Swift currents from the spring runoff made rescue efforts dangerous. Barton's entombed body was retrieved with the locomotive, but Sutton was missing. An attempt was made to recover Sutton's body by shooting a cable across the river at Cambrai. The cable had a number of sturgeon hooks attached to it, their purpose being to snag the floating body as it passed under the cable. But the cable caught nothing and Sutton's body was later recovered at Cedar Island, many miles downstream. Tragedy is not uncommon at this spot. Several fatal boating accidents have taken place at Boxcar. Perhaps one important factor is the unusual bedrock formation, which creates a whitewater flow that runs perpendicular to the river direction.*

Courtesy of J.C. Meyers

This accident gave this rapid its name.

The submerged boulder on the left side of Boxcar creates a wave of gigantic proportions. This wave probably turns more boats over than any other place on the river.

Rapid No.	Mileage	Class	
86	43.7	2+	**IDENTIFICATION:** Approximately 200 yards below No. 85. **HOW TO: Pass through in midriver, avoiding large standing waves which hide submerged boulders.**
87	44.2	2	**IDENTIFICATION:** Several small boulders on the left bank mark the beginning. **HOW TO: Position 1/3 off left bank and enter down center of V-slick. Look ahead to see an exposed midriver boulder which must be avoided at the lower end of the rapids. Ride out on the crests of standing waves.**
88	44.9	1+	**IDENTIFICATION:** Trees on river's edge on right bank; orange diamond-shaped wood-chip bin visible high on left slope; Maupin's bridge can be seen in the distance (about 1 mile ahead). **HOW TO: Approach slightly right of center to avoid rocks on left and right riverbed. Hold this position, moving slightly to left of center to avoid downstream rocks.**
—	45.2	1+	*COMMENTS: Cambrai railroad station on left.*
89	45.2	1+	**IDENTIFICATION:** Tom Allen Riffle — named for an early member of the Fly Fishers Club of Oregon. Cable supporting water pipe crosses river. **HOW TO: Position approximately 1/3 off right bank and pass through.**
90	45.6	1+	**IDENTIFICATION:** River bends to left; whitewater located about 200 yards above Maupin bridge. **HOW TO: Position 1/3 off right bank. Allow current to carry you across river to left bank. Pull off left bank and stay with standing waves to the end of the rapids.** *COMMENTS: About 150 yards below No. 90, the remains of the original old bridge piers can be seen on the right bank.*
—	45.8	—	*COMMENTS: Maupin City Park is on the right. Most drift trips end at this point. During summer months the pull-out ramp is very busy. By planning ahead, you can remove your craft quickly and conveniently without obstructing others behind you. A small fee is charged for each boat or craft removed from the river at this ramp.*
91	45.9	1	**IDENTIFICATION:** Located at Maupin boat landing. **HOW TO: Enter midriver V-slot and maintain this position through whitewater.**

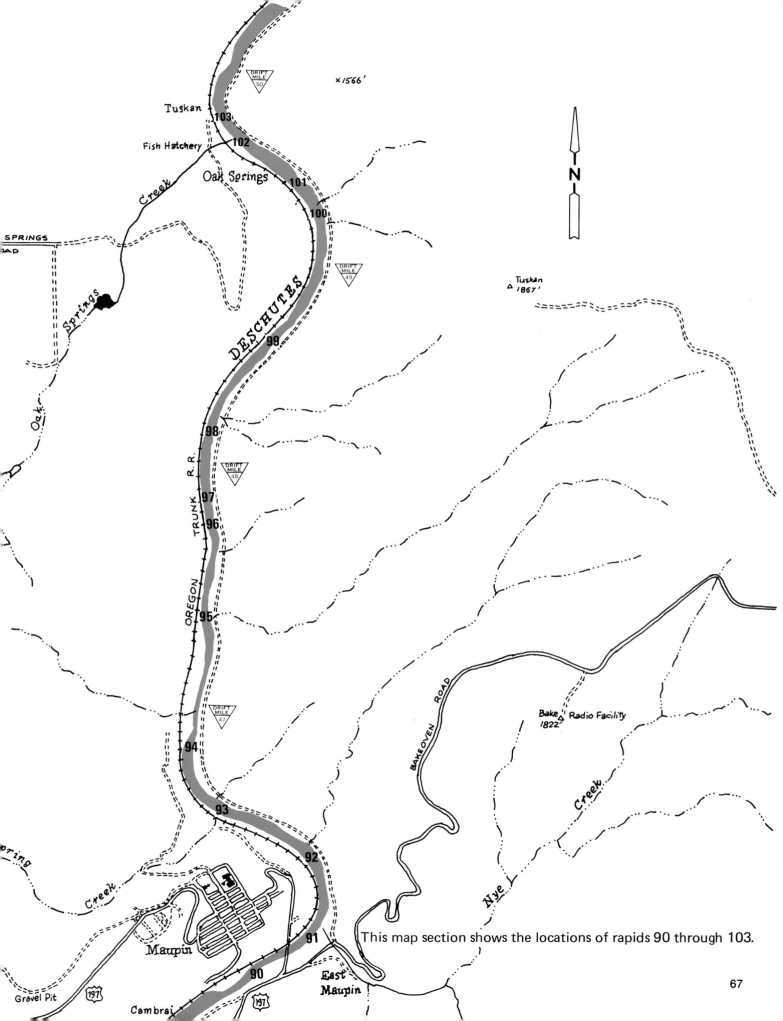

This map section shows the locations of rapids 90 through 103.

67

Aerial view of Maupin. The boat ramp is located just above the highway bridge on the east side of the river.

Running Conestoga

COMMENTS: Bakeoven Creek enters from the east bank. In 1862, Joseph Sherar was leading a party of miners eastward. Their evening camp was at a freshwater springs up Bakeoven Creek. Indians stole their horses in the night, leaving them with supplies, but no way of moving them. Sherar directed the party's cook to build an old-country oven to bake bread for the party. The rough clay and stone structure soon became a popular source of fresh bread for passing travelers. Eventually, an inn was built at the resting place, and it was given the name "Bakeoven Inn." A fire burned the inn to the ground and the only sign of the original stopover is a modern house located on today's 90,000+ acres of the Hinton and Ward Ranch. In 1880, a rugged Kentuckian, Howard Maupin, had established a ferry near the mouth of Bakeoven Creek. A few years later, Maupin sold the ferry to W.E. Hunt, who renamed it "Hunt's Ferry." W.H. Staats bought the townsite in preparation for the railroads which were to be built up the Deschutes canyon. Staats named the townsite "Maupin's Ferry," but postal authorities cut off the last word, and since 1909 the town has been called "Maupin."

Rapid No.	Mileage	Class	
92	46.1	2	IDENTIFICATION: 100 yards below No. 91; water pushes up on shallows and creates a gravel bar on the right.

HOW TO: Enter V-slot on left. Pass through on crests of standing waves.

| 93 | 46.6 | 2 | IDENTIFICATION: Flat on right bank. |

HOW TO: Position about 30 feet off right bank, and hold position through whitewater. Maneuver slightly to avoid downstream boulders.

COMMENTS: A campground is located on the right bank. It has picnic tables and toilets and should accomodate a large party nicely.

| 94 | 46.9 | 2+ | IDENTIFICATION: Powerline crosses river overhead; island splits river; main channel is to the left, but you want to take the right channel. |

HOW TO: Take right channel. Position approximately 20 feet off island. Once past island, ride out rapids on crests of medium standing waves for next several hundred yards.

COMMENTS: Shrubs on the left bank grow because of water seepage from gravel and porous lava which overlie the Columbia River basalt flows.

| 95 | 47.4 | 2 | IDENTIFICATION: Flat on left bank ends; river makes an S-turn ahead as it narrows. |

HOW TO: Position in midriver and ride small standing waves. Pull off left bank as river tries to push you into it. Maintain position on crests of small standing waves as you pass through the rapids.

| 96 | 47.7 | 1 | IDENTIFICATION: Right bank extends into river, causing narrows; old roadbed on left bank. |

HOW TO: Position in midstream and pass through minor riffle.

COMMENTS: *The old roadbed on the left bank is just one of many remnants of the railroad construction era. Roads like this were used to supply equipment to construction crews. Black powder was transported by surefooted mules, rather than by wagon, because of the roughness of the roads.*

Rapid No.	Mileage	Class	
97	47.9	1	IDENTIFICATION: Rocks protrude from left riverbed.

HOW TO: **Maintain position in midstream and pass through this minor riffle.**

| 98 | 48.7 | 2 | IDENTIFICATION: Several standing waves on left river surface mark beginning of whitewater. |

HOW TO: **Position in midriver at start; then move to within 50 feet of left bank to avoid midriver shallows extending from right bank.**

| 99 | 48.6 | 2 | IDENTIFICATION: River surface develops small whitecaps as river shallows on the right side. |

HOW TO: **Position 1/3 off left bank and maintain position through the rapids. Move to within 20 feet of left bank at lower section of rapids as river narrows severely.**

| — | 49.0 | — | COMMENTS: *A fishing ramp for the handicapped has been constructed on the right bank. It was developed by the Western Rod and Reel Club, Portland. The tail-out, just below the ramp for the handicapped, is a well-known steelhead spot known as the "Blue Hole."* |

| 100 | 49.2 | 1 | IDENTIFICATION: Standing wave in midriver as river begins to bend to left. |

HOW TO: **Pass by standing wave on left side for easy passage.**

| 101 | 49.4 | 2+ | IDENTIFICATION: Car ramp and park on right bank; small island in midstream. |

HOW TO: **Position in midriver. Pass within 10 feet of island on its left or right side. Below first island, position in midriver to avoid shallows in left midriver and on right side. Move left with main current to avoid severe shallowing caused by ledges extending into the river from both left and right riverbeds. Pass out of rapids by staying in right channel as final island splits river at bottom of rapids.**

| 102 | 49.8 | 2 | IDENTIFICATION: River bends to right; white building with aluminum roof on left at railroad tracks; several other buildings located up river bank on left side belong to the Oak Springs Fish Hatchery. |

HOW TO: **Position midriver and avoid standing waves by moving to left or right as necessary. River shallows on right, so move to left 1/3 to stay in main channel.**

This aerial view shows Oak Springs Rapids at high water.

103   49.9   4   *****SCOUTING MANDATORY***SCOUT FROM RIGHT BANK OR ROAD**

IDENTIFICATION: OAK SPRINGS RAPIDS — Starts approximately 100 yards below end of No. 102; concrete fish-rearing tanks can be seen several hundred feet from the river, up the left bank; two rock ridges in midriver identify the start of the rapids.

HOW TO: Hard boats should seriously consider lining around this rapids via the chute on the left bank. Competent raftsmen have a better chance of safely traversing this difficult piece of whitewater. To set up, position in midchannel and identify the two rock outcroppings which split the river into three channels. Hard boats take the left channel, lining in low water if necessary. Inflatables may choose the risky center channel. DON'T TAKE THE RIGHT CHANNEL! Once your craft is committed, position in middle of center channel and maneuver as necessary to avoid obstructions. Upon passing out of center channel's first turbulent introduction, IMMEDIATELY move to within 10 feet of the right bank to avoid several submerged rock ledges in midriver. After passing these obstructions, move quickly back to the left side of the river to re-enter the main channel as soon as possible. A rugged ledge of bedrock extends halfway across the river from the right bank and must be avoided. Once past this bedrock ledge, move quickly back to the right 1/3 of the river and pick your way past a number of small obstructions until you pass out of the rapids.

COMMENTS: Oak Springs was named because of the vegetation surrounding the fresh water springs and creek supplying the fish hatchery. A railway station named "Tuskan" is located on the left bank a short distance below the entry of Oak Springs Creek into the river. The term "tuskan" is derived from the Indian term "tusk-kan-ee," which referred to the locality near Sherars Bridge. Basalt in this area inclines northward, unlike the vertical orientation of the same basalt upstream where it forms the Mutton Mountains.

104   50.8   2+   IDENTIFICATION: River shallows on right; flat begins on right; White River railroad bridge approximately 1/4 mile ahead, on left.

HOW TO: Position 30 feet off left bank and hold position through the first 100 yards of the rapids. The river then shallows on the left side as the White River joins the Deschutes. Follow main current to the right side of the river and pass around the bend of the river by holding position within 20 feet of the right bank. Finally, rapids ends by current being forced to the left because of a basalt ledge on the right. Stay with the main current and pass into calmer waters below.

COMMENTS: The White River is the last large tributary of the Deschutes. The river is so named because of the glacial silt which it carries in flood stages. The source of the river is the White River Glacier on Mount Hood. The original Indian name, referred to in the journals of Lewis and Clark, was "Skimhoox River." H.E. Carlton built the first road down the White River canyon in 1909. Its purpose was to supply the materials used by railroad construction crews as they worked in this section of the canyon. Carlton's journal is the source of much of the data we will refer to as you continue your journey down the Deschutes. Approximately 1/4 mile after you have passed the mouth of the White River, look back over your shoulder to see a nice view of Mount Hood framed in the White River canyon.

Oak Springs is one of the most difficult rapids on the river.

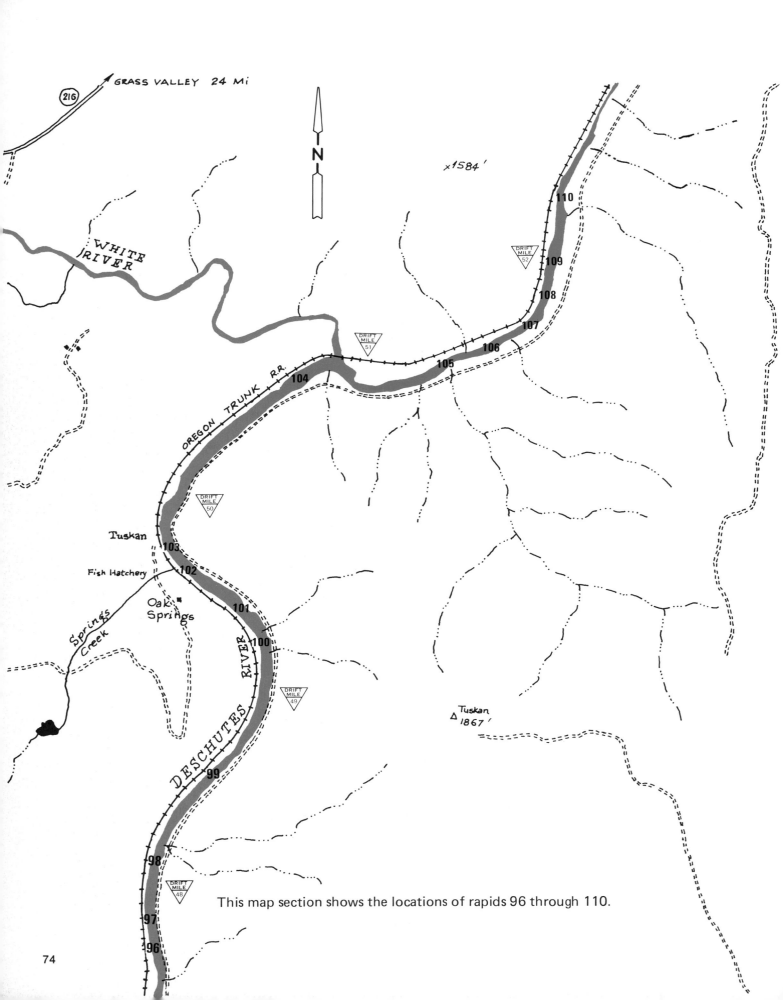

GRASS VALLEY 24 Mi

216

N

×1584'

WHITE RIVER

110

DRIFT
MILE
52

109

108

107

DRIFT
MILE
51

106

105

OREGON TRUNK R.R.

104

DRIFT
MILE
50

Tuskan

103

Fish Hatchery

102

Oak
Springs

101

100

Springs
Creek

DESCHUTES RIVER

DRIFT
MILE
49

Tuskan
△ 1867'

99

98

DRIFT
MILE
48

This map section shows the locations of rapids 96 through 110.

97

96

74

White River Falls is located 3 miles upstream from its mouth. The river drops over 90 feet.

Rapid No.	Mileage	Class	
105	51.3	2	IDENTIFICATION: River narrows, trees extend to river's edge on right bank; river shallows on right side.
			HOW TO: **Position approximately 30 feet off left bank and ride through on crests of standing waves.**
106	51.5	2	IDENTIFICATION: Concrete culvert under railroad tracks on left bank, about 100 yards before the rapids.
			HOW TO: **Position in midriver. Enter the center of the V-slot and ride out on the crests of medium standing waves. Avoid boulders on right.**
107	52.8	2	IDENTIFICATION: River narrows severely as it bends to left.
			HOW TO: **Position midstream and take main V-slot through narrow channel.**
108	51.9	2	IDENTIFICATION: Located approximately 150 yards downstream from No. 107; rock ledges entering from both left and right cause constriction of river.
			HOW TO: **Take center of V-slot through whitewater.**
109	52.0	2+	IDENTIFICATION: OSBORNE RAPIDS — Identify by locating midriver boulder.
			HOW TO: **Position in midstream and enter main V-slot. Pass boulder by taking left channel. Reposition about 10-15 feet off left bank and enter V-slot of next whitewater. Once through this chute, move to the right center to miss large boulder in midstream. Pass this boulder in the right 1/3 of the river, and hold position to avoid several other midstream rocks and islands. Be prepared for one final swift chute around the bend ahead. Several hundred yards downstream from its beginning, the rapids comes to an end and the river calms and widens.**
110	52.4	1+	IDENTIFICATION: Culvert under railroad tracks on left bank; large solitary pine tree on left bank; river narrows because of rock ledge extending from right bank.
			HOW TO: **Position in center of V-slot and ride through.**

COMMENTS: You now enter a very narrow canyon which has resulted from a massive brickbat basalt flow impeding the river. The canyon continues for the next 1/2 mile to the junction of White Water Creek. This junction marks the end of your safe passage on this section of the Deschutes. Within 200 yards, Sherars Falls makes further river passage impossible. A railroad bridge crosses highway 216 and White Water Creek enters on your left. To end your journey, you may either pull-out or portage. The best pull-out site is on the left side of the river about 100 yards above the Falls. To portage, move to the right side of the river and pull-out when the bank flattens to permit foot passage.

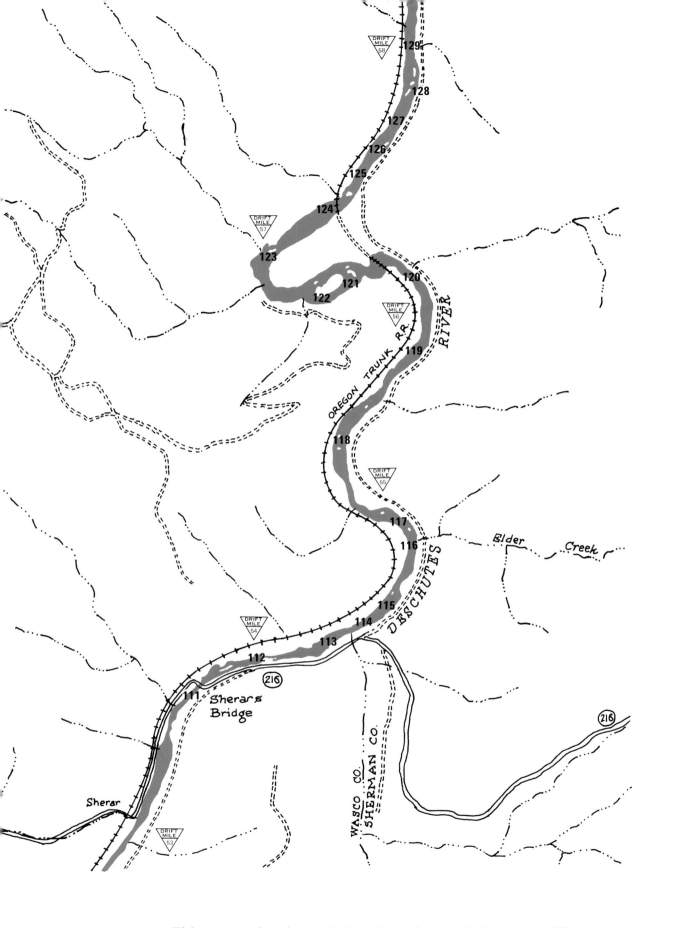

This map section shows the locations of rapids 111 through 129.

Indians still fish at Sherars Falls.

Mark Angel takes Sherar Falls in a Shoshoni Mark V.

Photo by Jim Miller

John Y. Todd build the first bridge across the Deschutes at this site.

This is an upstream view of the falls and fish ladder.

Sherars Bridge, the old gateway to central Oregon.

SHERARS FALLS — *The river plunges 15 feet over a basalt cliff. In 1826, Peter Skene Ogden followed an ancestral trail from the Columbia to this point. His journal says: "... we found an Indian camp of 20 families. Finding a canoe, also a bridge made of slender wood, we began crossing. 5 horses were lost through the bridge." In 1855, a ferry was built at this point by an Ohioan named Evelyn. His passengers were usually gold prospectors. With the outbreak of the Indian war, Evelyn deliberately sunk his ferry and it was never put back into service. Major Enoch Steen (after whom the Steen Mountains are named) designated Sherars Falls as the most likely military crossing. In 1860, John Todd built the first white man's bridge across the waterfall. In 1871, Joseph Sherar bought the bridge for $7,040. The bridge at Sherars Falls served as the link which joined the two largest cities in this part of Oregon (Canyon City on the John Day River, and The Dalles on the Columbia River). Millions of dollars worth of gold and mining supplies were carried over the bridge. Sherar charged $3.75 for each team and wagon, with $1 extra for the driver (the money was placed in large buckets at the ends of the bridge). Sherar used Indian labor to build $75,000 worth of roads within 30 miles on each side of his bridge. He also built a 13-room inn to serve traders, prospectors and travelers for many years. In 1912, Wasco County purchased the bridge for $3,000 and it was replaced by the present concrete bridge; the inn burned to the ground in 1940, and today only memories remain. A barn at Sherars Bridge was so tightly constructed there wasn't a single nail used to hold it together; rather, it was held together by hand-carved wooden pegs. There was adventure associated with the old bridge. In 1864, the Pony Express ran between Canyon City and The Dalles, covering 225 miles in 28 hours, and charging 50 cents per letter carried. On the second run, the Pony Express rider was attacked and shot by Indians. Also in this area, on Highway 26 near Mitchell, a monument marks the site of a stagecoach attack. Indians shot the stagecoach driver, Henry Wheeler, in the face. Wheeler and his passenger escaped by riding the stage team's lead horses, leaving the stage behind. When the Indians vandalized the coach, they ignored $10,000 in currency, choosing to take only the leather used in the harness and upholstery. This waterfall is an ancestral Indian fishing site. Today you will see modern Indians using dip-nets in the fashion of their ancestors. Celilo Indians (from the Columbia River ancestral fishing grounds) were forced to fish elsewhere after the construction of the Dalles Dam in 1965. Many of them moved up the Deschutes to fish here. On a good day in the spring or fall, up to 50 fish may be taken from the river by the Indians on the scaffolds. Fishing is restricted to members of the Confederated Tribes of the Warm Springs Reservation, and is for ceremonial and subsistence purposes only.*

Rapid No.	Mileage	Class
111	53.8	3

IDENTIFICATION: UPPER BRIDGE RAPIDS — Sherars Bridge is ahead some 150 yards; Sherars Falls is an equal distance behind. Only expert boatmen should attempt this rapids and Lower Bridge Rapids ahead!

HOW TO: Position in midstream to pass through V-slot of the chute above the bridge. Pass under the bridge and out of the narrow canyon in midchannel. Move straight ahead into the main V-slot forming between rocky ledges on both sides. Look ahead to identify a rock island with willows growing on it. Pass to the right of the island in midchannel. Hold position in the center of the standing waves. Avoid rocky shelves on both sides of the main channel as it winds its way through the rock strata in this section.

112   54.0   4+   ***SCOUTING MANDATORY*SCOUT FROM RIGHT BANK**

IDENTIFICATION: LOWER BRIDGE RAPIDS OR CONESTOGA RAPIDS — Identify a large rock spike which splits the river. Main channel goes left, but you must TAKE THE SMALLER RIGHT CHANNEL!

HOW TO: Take right channel. Enter V-slot, immediately pulling hard to hold position within 1 foot of the rock island. Hold position until approximately 50 feet along the island, then you must pull back HARD across the stream to the right bank so that you can hit the V-slot on the right side (and thereby avoid the pour-off from the boulders at the end of the island). Once past this major hazard, hold position near right center and pass into calmer water.

113   54.2   1   IDENTIFICATION: Rock shelf on left bank, river moves slightly to left; water develops minor chop as it takes gentle curve.

HOW TO: Maintain position in midriver as you pass through.

COMMENTS: Buck Hollow Creek enters from the right bank. This marks the boundary between Wasco and Sherman Counties. The boundary follows the creek into the middle of the Deschutes, and continues north to the Columbia. The west side of the river is Wasco County, the east side is Sherman County. A B.L.M. road can be seen on the east side of the river for the next 17 miles, ending at Macks Canyon.

114   54.4   1   IDENTIFICATION: Buck Hollow Creek enters from right; highway 216 bridge over Buck Hollow Creek; river narrows as rock walls form on both sides.

HOW TO: Maintain position in midriver for easy passage.

115   54.6   1   IDENTIFICATION: River bends to left; brushy knoll extends into river from the right; river shallows on right.

HOW TO: Position in left 1/3 of river and pass by shallows.

COMMENTS: A sandy clear site on the right bank is suitable for a put-in.

116   54.9   1   IDENTIFICATION: Culvert on right bank marks Elder Creek entry into the river.

HOW TO: Pass through in midriver.

117   55.0   1   IDENTIFICATION: Columnar vertical basalt patterns identify beginning of riffle.

HOW TO: Pass down center. No problem.

118   55.1   1+   IDENTIFICATION: Canyon narrows; basalt forms cake-layer pattern.

HOW TO: Enter approximately 40% off right bank. A steady whitewater chop extends several hundred yards around the bend. At the lower end of the riffle, turbulence increases. Midstream obstacles are avoided by staying within 30 feet of the right bank.

119   55.9   1   IDENTIFICATION: River bends to left; road is close to river on right; rock walls show signs of active waterfalls during rainy seasons.

HOW TO: Stay in midstream and ride minor whitewater chop.

COMMENTS: Tensions between the rival railroads developed short tempers and one hot summer day in 1909, Harry Carleton and his friend Albert Hill ran into several surveyors working for the Deschutes railroad. One of the surveyors, named Craven, badgered Carleton saying, "All you are is a mercenary, and a hired gunman brought in here to cause trouble." The hot-tempered Irishman quickly began the fistfight, which ended just as quickly as both men were quickly satisfied. During the fight Carleton heard his friend Hill say, "Don't any of you other guys horn in, this is a two man affair."   When Carleton looked around, he saw Hill holding the other surveyors off with a six-gun.

120   56.1   1+   IDENTIFICATION: Road on right begins upgrade; gravel bar on left.

HOW TO: Stay within 30 feet of the right bank. Pass out on crests of small standing waves.

COMMENTS: Remains of an old pier can be seen a few hundred feet below No. 118.

*CHECKPOINT
NO. 6
56.3

TWIN CROSSINGS (Upstream Crossing) — This is the only time you will see the railroad tracks on your right. When the 1909 construction efforts of the Oregon Trunk railroad crews (normally restricted to the west bank of the river only) reached a point downstream on the left bank (1.1 miles ahead, around the bend), they found an impassable rock wall. They requested and obtained permission to cross over to the east bank, drill a tunnel through the rock cliff you see in front of you, then cross back over to the west bank via the crossing which you see at this point. The two crossings which permitted this short detour to the east bank are called the "twin crossings" by railroad men. Although the tunnel is only a couple of hundred yards in length, it saves approximately 1.1 miles of roadbed. You will come to the lower of the two crossings as you continue drifting downriver. The bend in the river between the twin crossings used to be called "Horseshoe Bend" by oldtimers. However, today the term "Horseshoe Bend" is reserved for another, larger bend downstream some 10 miles from this point, at drift mile 66. Local guides refer to this area as "Twin Trestles" or "Horseshoe." As an example of the extremely competitive battle which existed between the two railroads in 1909, two tunnels were built through the solid rock wall on the right. Today only one tunnel remains in use (it is the one described above, used by the Oregon Trunk railroad). They were constructed by competing teams of laborers who used only blackpowder, picks and shovels and received the double-time wage of $5 per day. The tunnels were only 100 yards apart and tensions between the two competing companies ignited into frequent name-calling fistfights and rock-throwing free-for-alls. The tunnel used today was constructed by H.E. Carleton and his crew of 150 Italian laborers who followed Carleton to this project after working together for years on other railroad construction efforts around the United States. This area is also interesting because of the reports of Ted Lewis, track inspector for the Oregon Trunk railroad, which indicate this vicinity may have been the site of a ceremonial burial grounds for some primitive society.

Aerial view of "Twin Crossings" 70 years after Harry Carleton and his men built the tunnel.

Early tunnel construction in 1909.

Rapid No.	Mileage	Class	
121	56.5	2	**IDENTIFICATION:** Located approximately 150 yards below the railroad crossing; an island splits the river; either channel is passable; we chose the right channel. **HOW TO: Approach within 50 feet of the right bank in the right channel. Avoid standing waves in center. Hold position until out of this piece of whitewater. Look ahead to avoid obstacles and maneuver as necessary.**
122	56.6	1	**IDENTIFICATION:** Located approximately 150 yards downstream from No. 119, at the lower end of the island; identify a small standing chop. **HOW TO: Pass through in the center. No problem.**
123	56.9	2	**IDENTIFICATION:** River bends to right; midstream boulders; lower railroad bridge of "twin crossings" can be seen in distance. **HOW TO: Pass to right of large standing waves located in midstream. As current forces you into sheer rock walls, pull back to position on the center of the standing waves, and maintain position within 15 feet of the right bank.**
124	57.2	2	**IDENTIFICATION:** Approximately 100 yards above the railroad bridge ahead; the surface forms standing waves because of the pour-off from both banks; midstream submerged ledges must be avoided at the middle of the whitewater stretch. **HOW TO: Position slightly left of midstream to avoid midstream ledges and rock outcroppings. Whitewater continues to the railroad bridge. Hold position, maneuvering slightly to avoid obstructions.**

Safe passage at Wreck Rapids is along the left side of the river.

This head-on meet gave the rapids its name. Note the lone surviving horse on right.

Rapid No.	Mileage	Class
125	57.3	1

IDENTIFICATION: Located several hundred feet below the railroad bridge.

HOW TO: Pass midstream to avoid the shallows which develop on both sides of the river.

COMMENTS: Now that you have passed around the horseshoe-shaped bend between the "twin crossings" you can re-identify the B.L.M. road on the right bank. Its guard-rails can be seen some distance above the river.

126	57.6	3

SCOUTING MANDATORYSCOUT FROM LEFT BANK***

IDENTIFICATION: WRECK RAPIDS — Current is swift leading into this rapids, so be prepared for the extra force when you make your landing on the left bank to scout the rapids. To identify, you will see splashes and spouts of water ahead; river shallows on right as boulders encroach into the river; an island lies downstream, beyond the rapids.

HOW TO: After scouting, approach in left midstream. Angle to left to avoid rock shallows encroaching from right. Identify a rock point on the left bank at the entrance. Pass within a few feet of the suckhole created by the rock point. Enter the main V-slot and ride through on the crests of the large standing waves. Once through the rapids, stay in midriver and avoid obstacles as required. (Note: for the inexperienced, it is possible to line your boat down the right side.)

Courtesy of Ted Lewis

COMMENTS: *On September 22, 1949 a head-on collision between Engine 3128 (steam - northbound) and Engine 440 (diesel - southbound) occurred at this site. The two engines were to meet and pass at Oakbrook Station, several miles downstream. However, a miscalculation resulted in this tragic accident which left three dead. Engine 440 carried a number of horses at the time of the accident. All but one was either killed or injured severely. Injured horses were destroyed and cremated on the left bank. Occasionally, their sun-bleached bones are found by those who are scouting the rapids. The one horse which survived spent the rest of its time at the station-master's home in Maupin; it was named "Oregon Trunk."*

Rapid No.	Mileage	Class	
127	57.7	1	IDENTIFICATION: Located approximately 100 yards below No. 126.

HOW TO: Avoid whitewater by staying on left side of river, within 50 feet of the left bank.

| 128 | 57.9 | 1 | IDENTIFICATION: River flows off the right side shallows, towards left side. |

HOW TO: Pass through within 20 feet of left bank.

COMMENTS: *Several steel rails can be seen as reminders of the 1949 wreck. These rails vary in weight. Originally, they were 90 pounds per yard, today they weigh over 130 pounds per yard so that they can carry the heavier payloads hauled by the trains. One of the rails along the bank weighs approximately a ton, and is worth hundreds of dollars.*

129　58.0　1　　IDENTIFICATION: Located approximately 200 yards below No. 128; a midstream island splits the river.

HOW TO: Pass to right or left of island with no trouble.

COMMENTS: Interesting silt-and-talus slopes can be seen on the right bank. These slopes develop gullies and cuts because of erosion caused by torrential rain storms in this area. This type of erosion can be seen elsewhere on your river journey.

130　59.3　1　　IDENTIFICATION: Island in midstream splits river; main channel passes left.

HOW TO: The white chop extends for approximately 150 yards alongside the island. Remain near midchannel for simple passage.

COMMENT: A campsite can be seen on the right bank; garbage cans.

131　59.9　1　　IDENTIFICATION: Road runs close to river on right bank. Its cuts have been made through solid basalt.

HOW TO: Stay in right 1/3 of river channel. No problem.

132　60.3　1　　IDENTIFICATION: Gravel bar extends into river, causing narrowing and white-water.

HOW TO: Pass through in center of chute, remaining on tops of medium sized standing waves for a pleasant ride.

133　60.7　1　　IDENTIFICATION: Located approximately 200 yards beyond the end of No. 132; a flat is on the right side.

HOW TO: Pass down midstream through minor riffle. No problem.

COMMENTS: High on the left bank you can see columnar basalt and a natural bridge which has eroded through the uppermost layers. Rock pinnacles and cake-layer basalt make this a scenic passage. A petrified forest is on the upper levels of the strata on the east side. Present-day tropical and semi-tropical trees, such as acacia, ginkgo, cypress and teak once thrived in this area. Their petrified remains can be found because they have been exposed by the canyon which was cut by re-treating glaciers of the last ice age. Before the massive upheavals of the earth's crust had formed today's Cascade Mountain Range, this area was a tropical rain forest. There were no protective mountains to hold back the warm, moist marine air from the west. Constant rainfall and warm climates were responsible for lush vegetation, which permitted rhinoceros, mammoth, sabre-toothed tigers and many other prehistoric animals to exist. Their fossils are just being discovered in this immediate area today.

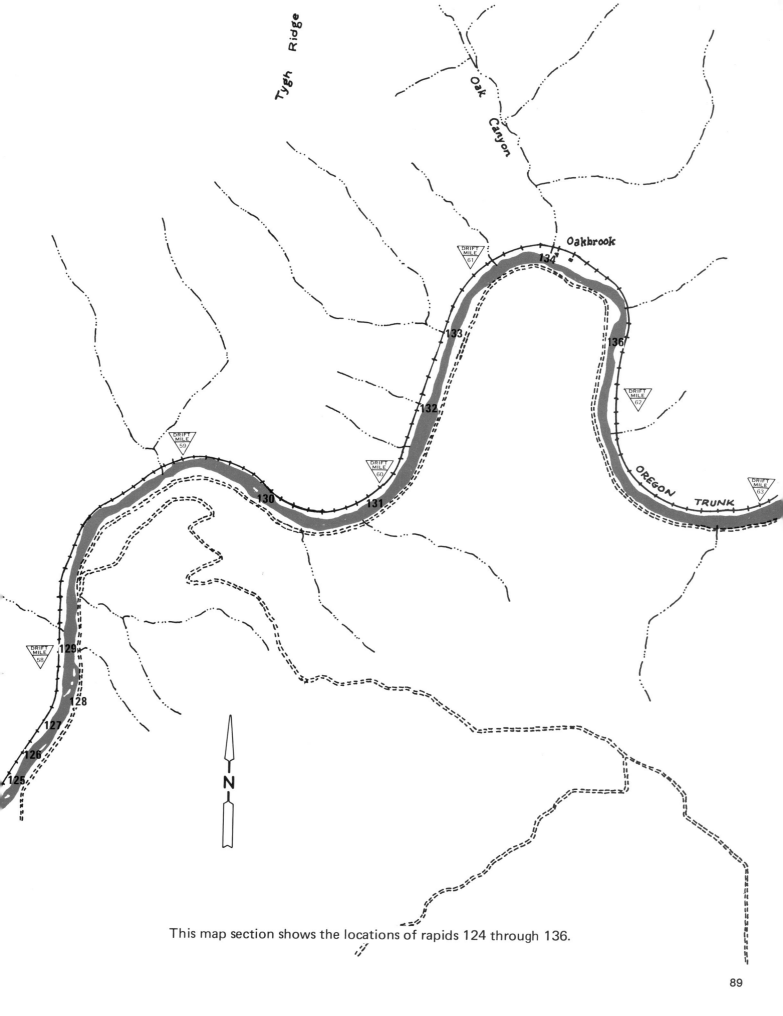

Tygh Ridge

Oak Canyon

Oakbrook

DRIFT MILE 61

134

133

136

132

DRIFT MILE 62

DRIFT MILE 59

DRIFT MILE 60

130

131

OREGON TRUNK

DRIFT MILE 63

DRIFT MILE 58

129

128

127

126

125

N

This map section shows the locations of rapids 124 through 136.

Rapid No.	Mileage	Class	
134	61.2	1	**IDENTIFICATION:** Two small railroad maintenance buildings mark the passing track at Oakbrook Station; Oak Canyon opens on the west bank.

HOW TO: Pass down the center of small standing waves, within 15 feet of the right bank.

COMMENTS: Oak Brook is the name of the creek in the canyon bearing that name. The brook was named because of the large number of oak trees which thrive along its banks. This site was also used as a large railroad construction camp in the early 1900's. Remains of the access road to the camp can still be seen carved into the west canyon wall. According to J. C. Meyers, this area also was used as an engine turning "wye" which enabled incoming engines to change direction to head back out of the canyon. In the 1950's, a fatal shooting occurred at this site. On payday, a night watchman went to Maupin "to get his nose wet." When he returned he was in a cantankerous mood and he began to abuse his wife. As the argument persisted, the drunken man handed his wife a 410-gauge shotgun and dared her to shoot him. She did — he died — no charges were filed — end of story. A head-on collision occurred just north of the Oakbrook passing track at 11 a.m., February 1, 1945. Southbound engine 2030, with engineer Harper and conductor Delaney, was traveling only 10 miles per hour when it collided with northbound engine 507, carrying engineer Cochran and conductor Lewis. Engine 507 was traveling about 20 miles per hour. Two men were killed in the accident. The next day, another fatality occurred as a carload of replacement rails arrived to rebuild the damaged tracks. The flatcar carrying the rails struck a rock on the track just a few hundred feet from here. The load shifted and crushed a workman as they fell from the car. Also, about 1,000 feet north of Oakbrook passing track, two carloads of Sherman tanks were derailed. One of the tanks rolled into the river, leaving only its gun-barrel visible. There is an ancient Indian burial grounds a short distance up Oak Canyon. Federal law prohibits disturbance and removal of artifacts found along the river. Do not violate these laws.

135	61.7	1	**IDENTIFICATION:** Campsite on right, suitable for large party (toilets); river bends to right.

HOW TO: Small standing waves in left center permit easy passage and an enjoyable ride.

136	61.9	1	**IDENTIFICATION:** Located just below the campsite described at No. 135; water pushes from the left into the right bank.

HOW TO: Stay within 30 feet of the right bank.

Comments: Massive vertical cliffs of basalt on the right bank create a dramatic passage. Pale green lichen streaks the surface of the basalt. On the left bank you can see the remains of the original construction road on the slopes above the railroad track. The roadbuilders built dyke-like rock foundations to span the shallow creeks and gullies. These roadbed foundations appear to be small dams which may protect the railroad track from erosion.

Aerial view of the "beavertail" and Cedar Island.

In 1909 both of the rival railroads had construction camps located in this area.

Rapid No.	Mileage	Class	

137   63.1   1   IDENTIFICATION: River narrows and shallows form on right half; bar extends out from right bank.

HOW TO: **Stay within 30 feet of the left bank and avoid midstream submerged boulders and shallows.**

COMMENTS: Jones Canyon opens on the east bank. Campsite on right.

138   63.3   1   IDENTIFICATION: River bends to left; gravel bar extends into river from left.

HOW TO: **Stay in approximate midstream and ride gentle whitewater.**

139   63.6   1   IDENTIFICATION: Sloping east bank is covered with sagebrush.

HOW TO: **No problem, pass through in the center.**

COMMENTS: Approximately 200 yards below No. 139 there is a campsite with nice shade trees and picnic tables. Also, a worktrain carrying ballast had a wreck along this section of the river.

140   64.6   1   IDENTIFICATION: Road ascends hill on right bank and curves to the left.

HOW TO: **Whitewater can be avoided altogether by staying in left center of the river, or a ride on small standing waves is possible by moving to right center.**

141   65.0   1+   IDENTIFICATION: River bends to the left.

HOW TO: **Position in left 1/4 of the river to avoid midstream bedrock. Maintain position by pulling towards left bank as current tries to force you to the right side of the river. This enables you to avoid rock outcroppings in the right half of the riverbed when you reach the lower half of the whitewater.**

COMMENTS: Railroad men refer to this point as the beginning of "Horseshoe Curve." The river makes a horseshoe-shaped turn around basalt cliffs on the east bank. The peninsula created by the large bend has also been given the name "The Beavertail" by river guides because of its resemblance to the flattened, horseshoe-shaped tail of a beaver.

142   65.7   1   IDENTIFICATION: A small island splits the river; either channel is passable.

HOW TO: **The left channel contains greater flow. If you take the left channel, stay in the left 1/3 of the channel to avoid midchannel shallows. Then move to midchannel to pass through whitewater. If you take the right channel, stay within 10 feet of the right bank to avoid severe shallowing at the end of the island.**

COMMENTS: There is a large campsite on the right bank within a few hundred feet downstream from No. 142. It is located on a large, sandy bar at the foot of the island and it has tables and toilets. Also, evergreen junipers and pine in this area mark the first coniferous trees visible on your drift down the lower Deschutes. Two brickbat basalt flows can be seen about halfway up the west bank across from the campsite. This has been described as one of the most picturesque and interesting basalt flows in the Deschutes canyon. On the east bank, examples of pillow lava can

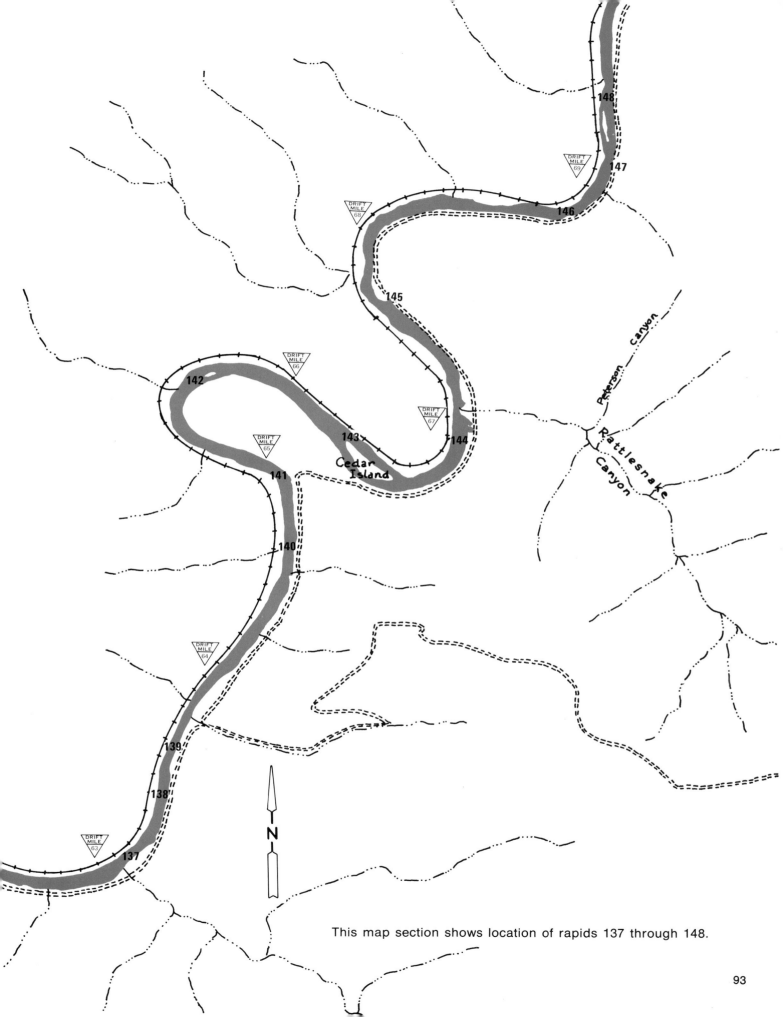

148

DRIFT
MILE
69

147

DRIFT
MILE
68

146

145

Peterson Canyon

142

DRIFT
MILE
66

Rattlesnake

DRIFT
MILE
67

Canyon

143

144

141

DRIFT
MILE
65

Cedar
Island

140

DRIFT
MILE
64

139

138

137

DRIFT
MILE
63

N

This map section shows location of rapids 137 through 148.

be identified. During railroad construction days, a large boulder was rolled down on an Oregon Trunk worktrain in this section. Retaliation was in order. That evening, as the Deschutes Railroad construction crew slept soundly in their tents on the flat on the right bank, an alert watchman discovered a sputtering fuse which led to a keg of black powder in the center of the camp. He was able to stamp out the fuse before an explosion occurred, but many of the crew left anyway, and it took weeks to rebuild the workforce. The next evening, all survey markings were obliterated on the west bank, forcing a completely new survey. Similar delay tactics were common for the duration of the railroad war up the canyon.

Rapid No.	Mileage	Class
143	66.4	2

IDENTIFICATION: Cedar Island splits the river and identifies the north end of "The Beavertail." Both channels are passable. Shallows develop at the lower end of the island.

HOW TO: Left channel: pass through choppy whitewater, avoiding protruding rocks and midstream boulders. Carefully pick your path through the shallows at the bottom end of the island. Right channel: smaller, but easier to pass through. It also has shallows at the lower end of the island which must be carefully picked through.

COMMENTS: Cedar Island is named because of the large incense cedar trees which grow on it. This is one of the few places in the lower Deschutes canyon where these moisture loving evergreen trees can grow. Cedar Island used to be the site of a famous great blue heron rookery, but the increased human traffic along the river has forced them to move downstream to the high cliffs away from the river's edge. The vacant nests and resting spots are now occupied largely by turkey vultures. On the right bank there is a large campsite suitable for automobile travelers.

144	67.0	2

IDENTIFICATION: Rattlesnake Canyon opens on the east bank, below the rapids.

HOW TO: Enter this rapids by positioning 1/3 off the left bank. Maintain this position until you reach the end of the rapids. Near the end of the rapids, move to midstream to avoid rock outcroppings and submerged boulders located approximately 20 feet off the left bank.

COMMENTS: Rattlesnake Campground can be seen on the right bank. It extends along the river's edge on both sides of the canyon. It is a large campsite and can accomodate many people. Toilets, garbage cans and picnic tables are available.

145	67.7	1

IDENTIFICATION: A gravel bar extends into the river from the right bank; interesting basalt formations on the right bank, approximately 300 yards before No. 145.

HOW TO: Position in midstream to avoid shallows on right. Ride through on medium standing waves.

COMMENTS: The Panama Canal and the Oregon Trunk railroad on the west bank were both built under the direction of the same engineer. His name was John F. Stevens. The secrecy and rivalry between the competing railroads, which fought to be the first to complete the Deschutes river passage to Bend, can be illustrated by

John Stevens.

this example of deception: Along this part of the river, an avid fisherman appeared in 1906. He carried an unusual amount of tackle. The stranger appeared at the various isolated stock ranches and introduced himself as "John Sampson." He appeared to be a wealthy sportsman on a fishing expedition. He would tell each rancher that he was having the time of his life and that he was interested in purchasing a small part of the rancher's land for his own personal enjoyment. He spent several months moving up and down the river, accumulating options to purchase much land along the Deschutes. Then the stranger left as suddenly and mysteriously as he had appeared. When the man dropped his disguise, he was John F. Stevens, the same man who President Theodore Roosevelt had asked to direct the United States' efforts to construct the Panama Canal. James Hill, the empire builder of Great Northern Railroad fame, considered Stevens to be the best construction engineer in the world. In 1889, in the dead of winter, Stevens discovered Marias Pass, the gateway through the Rocky Mountains which saved over 100 miles of track and gave Hill's Great Northern Railroad Company the lowest grade to the Pacific. Even after his Indian guides had turned back in the face of -40° temperatures, Stevens continued his successful search alone, on foot in uncharted hostile territory. Indeed, Stevens was a man of steel. Hill anticipated the difficulties of the race up the Deschutes canyon and he knew he needed a man of Stevens' talents if his company was to be the winner. Stevens' deception enabled the Oregon Trunk to purchase valuable right-of-way and thereby control strategic points along the river.

Rapid No.	Mileage	Class	
146	68.8	1	IDENTIFICATION: Several midstream boulders cause minor whitewater on left half of the river; interesting columnar basalt patterns at roadway on right.
			HOW TO: Boulders are easily avoided by maneuvering as necessary.
147	69.0	2	IDENTIFICATION: River drops over shelf; boulders cause midstream standing waves.
			HOW TO: Position approximately 1/3 off left bank and pass through.
148	69.1	1	IDENTIFICATION: Island on left side, take right channel.
			HOW TO: Position 1/3 off right bank and pass through on minor standing waves.

COMMENTS: During railroad construction days, the Oregon Trunk employed over 3,000 men, and the Deschutes Railroad had over 3,800 on its payroll. Approximately 15,000 pounds of fresh beef was consumed each day by the hungry workers. Good food was an essential part of each crew's daily existence. As a result, many incidents are reported of harassment of competitor's livestock herds by stampeding and disruption of the huge herds which grazed on the plateaus above the canyon. Artificial hay "shortages" were created as entire local feedstocks were deliberately bought out by the rival railroads.

Carleton's Camp No. 1 was located on a bluff above the Deschutes River.

Each time a train passes, the drifter is reminded of the great railroad battle that took place 70 years ago.

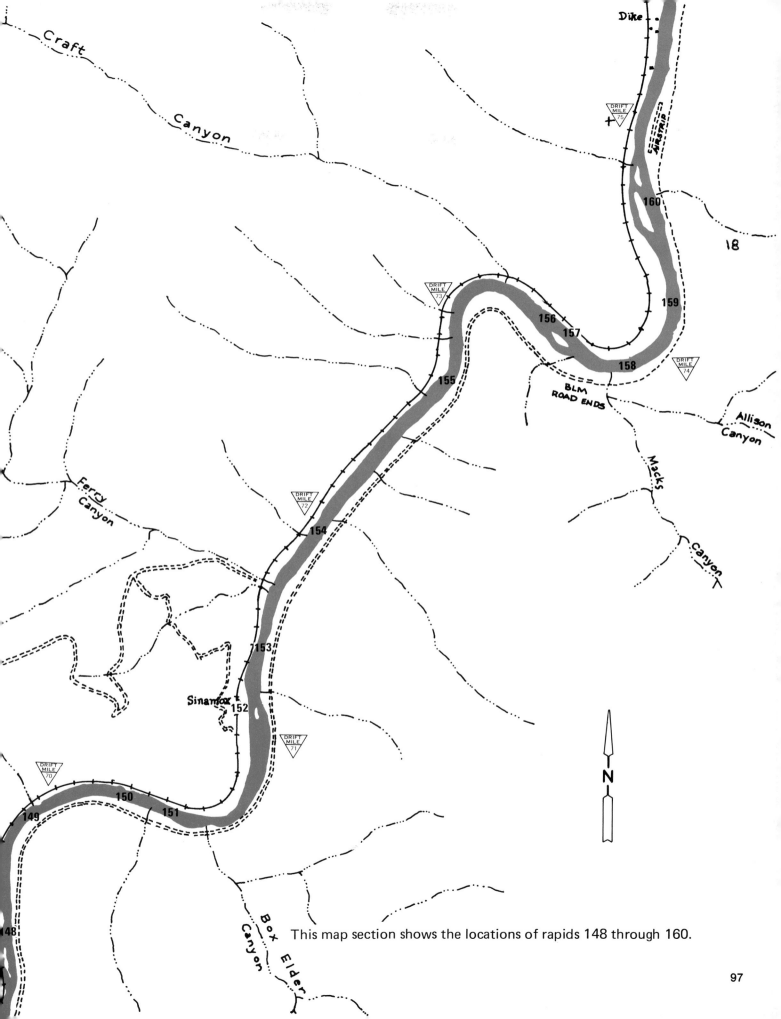

Dike

Craft

Canyon

DRIFT MILE 75

AIRSTRIP

160

18

159

DRIFT MILE 73

156

157

155

158

DRIFT MILE 74

BLM ROAD ENDS

Allison

Canyon

Ferry

Canyon

DRIFT MILE 72

154

Macks

Canyon

153

Sinanfox

152

DRIFT MILE 71

DRIFT MILE 70

150

N

149

151

Box Elder

Canyon

This map section shows the locations of rapids 148 through 160.

148

Rapid No.	Mileage	Class	
149	69.9	1	IDENTIFICATION: River bends gently to right, campsite on right bank. **HOW TO: To avoid minor whitewater on left side, pass midriver.**
150	70.1	1	IDENTIFICATION: Identify by small standing wave in midstream; a flat begins on the right bank. **HOW TO: Pass on either side of the small standing wave and ride out the minor riffle which results.**
151	70.4	1	IDENTIFICATION: Small caboose-shaped building and aluminum trailer on right bank. A row of old wooden railroad cars lines the road alongside the river. A good campsite can be seen on the right bank. **HOW TO: Position 30-40 feet off the left bank to avoid gravel bar on the right riverbed.** *COMMENTS: The old wooden railroad cars were left in this area when this section of the Deschutes railroad was abandoned in 1935. Today they are still used by fishermen and travelers. This site used to be called Hill's Ranch, and the remains of an abandoned ferry crossing can still be seen.*
—	70.6	—	*COMMENTS: Box Elder Canyon opens on east bank.*
CHECKPOINT NO. 7 71.1			*SINAMOX — "Sinamox" is the Chinook Indian jargon word for the number "seven." It was so named because it was the seventh station from the north end of the Oregon Trunk railway's junction with the Columbia. Sheep ranching activities were possible in this area because of the gentle grazing slopes on both sides of the river. Sinamox developed the reputation of being a major lambing and wool production center. Ferries were used to transport animals, equipment and men back and forth across the river. Remains of a ferry dock can be seen on the left bank. There is also a black powder storage cave on the west bank, used by the Oregon Trunk railroad in 1909. A railroad accident occurred here because of a "sun-kink" in the rails. When the heat of the extra hot sun expands the rails so that they consume all their engineered expansion space between rail-ends, continued expansion causes the rails to buckle or "kink." In the accident which resulted here, 11 cars and a caboose were derailed.*
152	71.1	1	IDENTIFICATION: River broadens and shallows on right; Sinamox Island in midstream splits river; take left channel. **HOW TO: Pass through in midchannel.**
153	71.4	1	IDENTIFICATION: Located at the lower end of Sinamox flat on the left bank. **HOW TO: The small whitecaps provide a gentle ride if you remain in midriver.**
—	71.7	—	*COMMENTS: Ferry Canyon opens on the west side of the Deschutes. Once again, this was the site of a ferry used to transfer food, equipment and livestock. Old buildings can be seen on the west side, a railroad trestle spans Ferry Canyon and green pastures are located on the canyon's slopes.*

Photo by Don Turcke

Make sure your gear is securely tied down and covered before entering whitewater.

154 71.8 1   IDENTIFICATION: Located approximately 300 yards downstream from Ferry Canyon.

HOW TO: Pass through in midriver.

155 72.8 1   IDENTIFICATION: River swings to right side.

HOW TO: Position in center and pass through with no problem.

COMMENTS: *A campsite can be identified on the left side. Another few hundred yards brings you to Macks Canyon Public Campground on the right bank. This large campground has toilets, picnic tables, firepits, garbage cans and a boat ramp.*

156 73.4 1   IDENTIFICATION: Macks Canyon Public Campground is still on the right; riffle forms on the left half of the river.

HOW TO: This minor riffle can be skirted by staying in the center of the river.

157 73.7 1+   IDENTIFICATION: Island splits river; main channel passes left; island located at the end of Macks Canyon Public Campground.

HOW TO: Enter left channel. As the river shallows, position slightly left of midstream for 150 yards of gentle whitecaps.

COMMENTS: *The foundation of an old railroad trestle on the east bank marks the end of the B.L.M. road which has followed the Deschutes from Buck Hollow Creek. It is interesting to consider that of all the miles of roadway which parallel the river, less than 1 mile is not built upon the remains of the old railway bed. The foundation of an old house can be seen on the left bank.*

158 73.9 1   IDENTIFICATION: Macks Canyon opens on the right; river narrows 50 yards downstream and forms an easy strip of whitewater.

HOW TO: Pass through with no trouble.

COMMENTS: *Macks Canyon is the site of numerous archeological finds. Fossils are commonly found on both sides of the Deschutes canyon at this point. Studies are constantly underway and fenced-off areas are visible. Please do not disturb these study sites. The fossils of this area were so numerous that they were first noted by early explorers and travelers. Thomas Condon, pastor of the First Congregational Church of The Dalles and founder of the Geology Department at the University of Oregon, studied these deposits in the 1860's and '70's. Oregon Trunk track inspector, Ted Lewis, recollects that when the Union Pacific steamed to Shaniko, if you listened very carefully along this stretch, you could hear the shrill sound of the whistle as it traveled down Macks Canyon.*

This was the only steam shovel used in building the railroads up the Deschutes Canyon.

159   74.0   1   IDENTIFICATION: River continues bend to left; a flat is evident on the west side.

HOW TO: Position in midstream for easy passage through whitewater.

COMMENTS: *Although the original tracks are gone, railroad ties still remain on the east bank. Also, on the west bank you can see the rock foundation of a black powder storage house used by the Oregon Trunk. The animosity between the two competing railroads led to raids across the river. One of the prime targets for the raids was the black powder supplies. Guards were posted around the powder houses to prevent surprise attacks in the night. The construction along the Deschutes canyon was the last black powder blasting project in the United States. Since 1910, dynamite and more sophisticated explosives have replaced the unpredictable black blasting powder. Near this point, the Deschutes Railroad made a final attempt at using steam shovels instead of handwork. They dismantled the massive equipment and lowered it piece by piece, using ropes, over the canyon walls to river level. Once down, the pieces were reassembled, but the effort was futile because the unique rock structure of the Deschutes canyon walls simply was not the type of rock which could be broken and handled by steam-powered equipment.*

160   74.6   1   IDENTIFICATION: Island splits river; main channel on right.

HOW TO: Follow right channel to the end of the first island, and then work left to pass between the first island and the second island.

COMMENTS: *On the flat on the east bank, between the river and the old railroad grade, the remains of an old airstrip can still be identified.*

Rapid No.	Mileage	Class

— 75.2 — COMMENTS: *Rusted gears and machinery can be seen on the west bank approximately 100 yards upstream from Dike. These are the remains of a pumping station used to supply water from the river to passing steam locomotives.*

— 75.3 — COMMENTS: *Several small railroad buildings, an outdoor toilet and a garbage disposal site mark the passing track on the west bank called "Dike." Just below Dike, the mouth of Sixteen Canyon opens on the east bank. Camping sites can be seen on the right bank. Dike was named for a topographical characteristic of this area.*

161 75.9 1 IDENTIFICATION: This gentle riffle begins at the opening of Sixteen Canyon and continues, gradually becoming more significant downstream, to the mouth of Dry Canyon.

HOW TO: Easy passage in midstream.

COMMENTS: *On the east bank, just above the island, a good campsite with B.L.M. toilets can be found. The rock foundations of an early railroad construction campsite can be seen. Also, on the west bank, just below the island, a campsite and the remains of another old railroad camp can be found.*

162 76.9 1 IDENTIFICATION: River bends to the left and narrows to form whitewater.

HOW TO: Pass through on the center of the standing waves for an enjoyable passage.

COMMENTS: *There is an excellent example of columnar basalt which has broken away from the canyon wall on the east bank. Rockfalls of this type were a constant worry to engineers traveling this stretch of the canyon. A small campsite can be seen on the gravel bar at the end of this riffle.*

163 77.0 2 IDENTIFICATION: Islands divide river into 3 channels. Take right channel.

HOW TO: Position within 20 feet of the right bank; at lower end of the island move to the left side of the channel to rejoin the other currents. Pass out of rapids in midstream.

COMMENTS: *There is a good campsite at the entry of No. 163. Approximately 400 yards below No. 163 there is an impressive example of vertical columnar basalt on the right bank. The 25-foot high basalt face extends to the water's edge.*

164 77.7 1+ IDENTIFICATION: River shallows severely on the left 80% of the river; also, river bends to the left.

HOW TO: Position within 20 feet of the right bank and follow standing waves around the bend of the river. Move back to midstream at lower end of whitewater.

COMMENTS: *Approximately 150 yards below No. 164 there is an alder-protected campsite on the grassy east bank.*

— 78.3 — COMMENTS: *A good example of columnar basalt that has been oriented horizontally to resemble a deck of petrified logs is visible on the bank. There is a small campsite under this formation. Also, river guide Oscar Lange has observed small airplanes landing on the west bank in this area.*

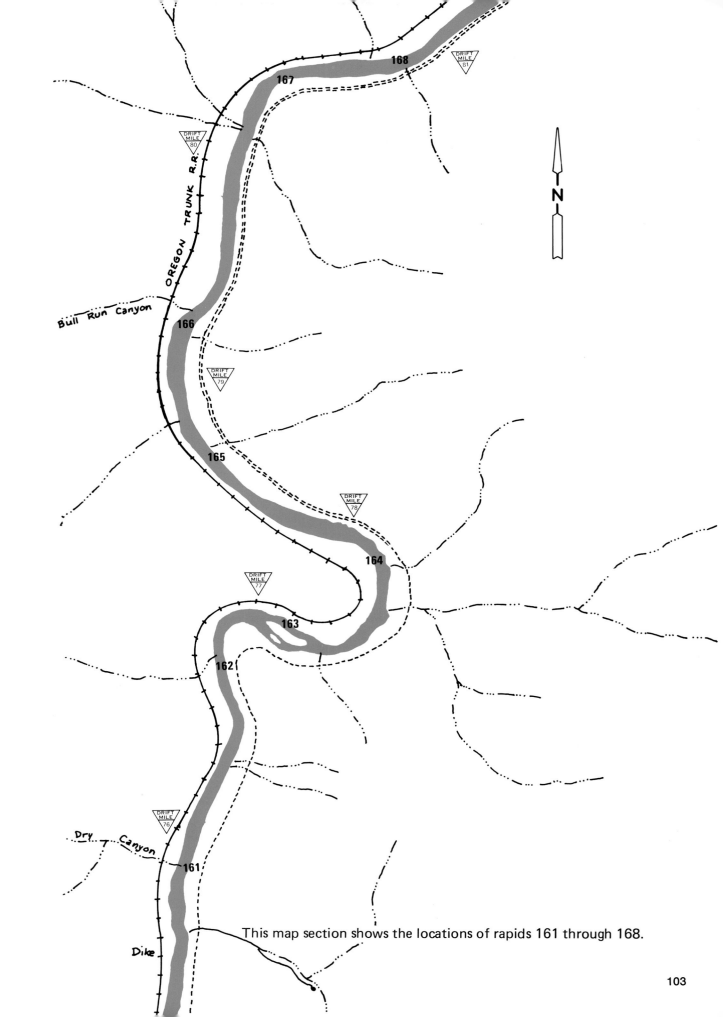

This map section shows the locations of rapids 161 through 168.

165   78.4   1   IDENTIFICATION: A flat is located on the right bank and the river narrows.

HOW TO: Stay in midstream and avoid submerged boulder on left side at entry.

166   79.2   2   IDENTIFICATION: Bull Run Rapids — Bull Run Canyon opens on the west bank below the rapids; the river shallows severely; main channel is on left half of the river.

HOW TO: Move to left of center and hold position down to the lower end, where large standing waves offer an exciting ride. Watch for submerged rock at end of rapids, near left center streambed.

COMMENTS: About 400 yards below Bull Run Rapids on the flat on the west side there is a chemical toilet.

—   80.1   —   *COMMENTS: Power line crosses river. This site on the Deschutes is referred to as the "Power Line Hole."*

167   80.2   1   IDENTIFICATION: Located approximately 200 yards below the power line; river bends to the right; flat appears on right bank; boulder bar extends into river from the right.

HOW TO: Enter whitewater in the center of the river and pull off the left bank to remain in midstream. Ride out whitewater on standing waves.

168   80.8   1   IDENTIFICATION: Railroad-car cabin on right bank; "No Trespassing" signs.

HOW TO: Stay in midstream; no problem.

169   81.7   1   IDENTIFICATION: River narrows slightly.

HOW TO: Stay within 40 feet of the left bank to pass through this riffle easily.

COMMENTS: A large railroad construction camp is located on the left bank just below No. 169. You can see the traces of roadway and tent-building foundations on the flat site. Several rock ovens are still recognizable, even though they have not been used for over 70 years. Construction roadbeds parallel the railroad tracks. Whenever grassy slopes were present, railroad camps were deliberately located next to the river's edge. This tactic was used to combat incendiary fires which might be set by the opposing railroad.

170   82.0   2   IDENTIFICATION: River shallows severely on right half.

HOW TO: Stay in left center to avoid rock outcroppings from left bank. Pass through on crests of medium standing waves in center of river channel.

COMMENTS: Large cement culvert pieces lie several hundred yards below No. 170. They appear to have fallen off a train. Also, remains of the old wagon roadbed can still be seen running next to the river on the west bank.

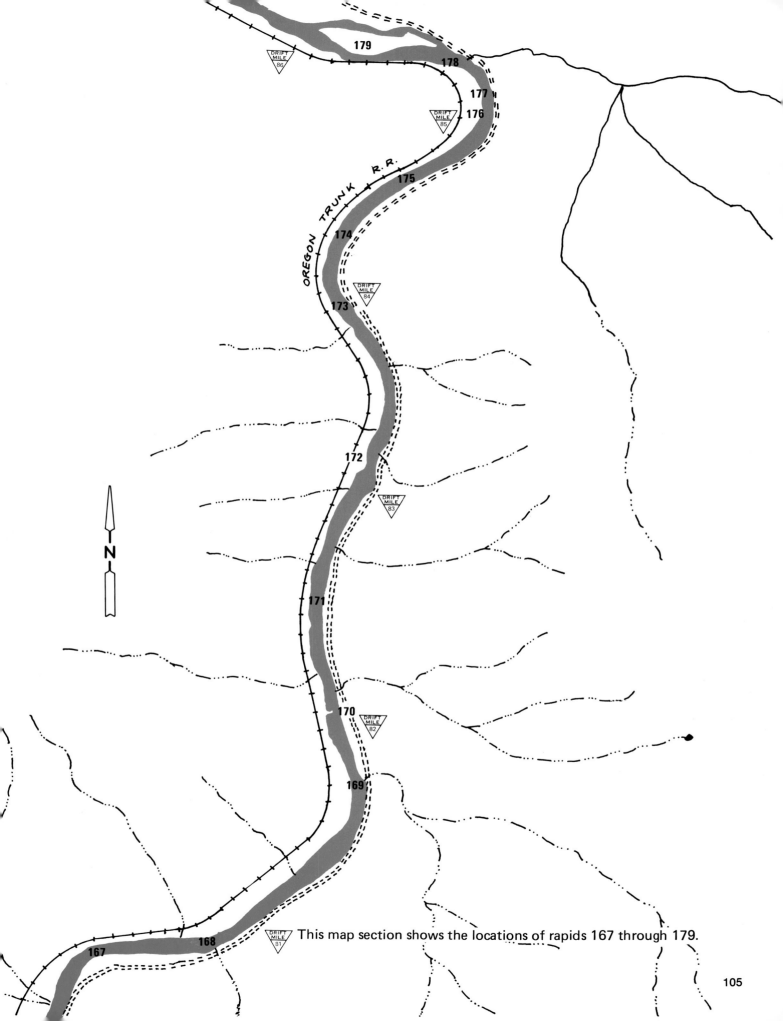

179

DRIFT
MILE
86

178

177

DRIFT
MILE
85

176

175

OREGON TRUNK R.R.

174

DRIFT
MILE
84

173

172

DRIFT
MILE
83

171

N

170

DRIFT
MILE
82

169

This map section shows the locations of rapids 167 through 179.

168

DRIFT
MILE
81

167

171   82.4   1   IDENTIFICATION: Rock outcropping on left bank.

HOW TO: Stay in midstream to avoid outcropping.

COMMENTS: An old boxcar on the right bank has a sign reading: "No Hunting. Private Land" painted in white letters. White alder lines the banks of both sides of the river. The old railbed follows the river on the east bank, exposing bridges and foundation structures periodically. At this site there is a story about the time the Deschutes Railroad track-laying crew worked all day to lay a beautiful stretch of shining steel. The next day they were dismayed to find their fresh trackage completely covered with rock rubble from the rival crew (across the river) which had blasted all night. In narrow areas of the canyon, the explosions would throw rocks several hundred yards through the air, across the river, to the other side.

172   83.1   1   IDENTIFICATION: Flat develops on left bank; river shallows on both sides.

HOW TO: Pass down center of whitewater.

COMMENTS: This section of track was cleared by blasting through the winter of 1910. The blasting technique is interesting. Holes were dug into the solid basalt by handwork (i.e. picks and shovels). These holes were approximately two feet in diameter and three or four feet in depth. They were called "coyote holes." Once dug, they were filled with black powder and the crews were ordered to clear the area before detonation. Following one such operation in this area, a solid ball of hundreds of writhing rattlesnakes was found by the construction crew when they returned to clear the rubble. The weather was cold and the snakes had gathered together for warmth. That evening, the crew's entertainment consisted of stealthily rowing across the river to the rival construction crew's sleeping quarters, where surprise "gifts" in burlap sack wrappings were left squirming and wriggling near the warm wood stoves. As a result, many of the Italian workers packed their gear and left as soon as possible.

173   83.9   1   IDENTIFICATION: Lockit passing tracks on left bank.

HOW TO: Remain in midstream for simple passage.

COMMENTS: "Lockit" is the Chinook jargon word for "four." This is the fourth station from the north terminus of the Oregon Trunk. Several serious railroad accidents have occurred within a short distance, both north and south, of Lockit's passing track.

174   84.1   1   IDENTIFICATION: Located approximately 200 yards below Lockit.

HOW TO: Remain in midstream for simple passage.

175   84.7   1   IDENTIFICATION: High basalt cliffs on left bank; a cave can be seen.

HOW TO: Pass midstream through this gentle riffle.

Coyote blast.

In 1910 this young lady and her family lived on the Harris homestead and raised sheep. Less than a mile from her tranquil surroundings, men of steel fought for control of an empire.

107

176　85.0　1　IDENTIFICATION: River shallows across width.

HOW TO: Remain midstream for simple passage.

COMMENTS: An interesting small storage shed is located on the roadside of the right bank. It was constructed of wood salvaged from the original railroad water tower which served the trains as they traveled through this area. Iron bands, used to hold the water tower's vertical planking in place, left scars on the wood and these scars can still be seen on the planking used inside the shed.

177　85.1　1　IDENTIFICATION: River shallows on left; small standing waves appear as river bends to left.

HOW TO: Pass through on crests of small standing waves as river bends to left.

COMMENTS: Campsite on left bank. Dramatic cathedral-like lava and basalt cliffs tower over the river. The powerful erosive actions of our last ice age's receding glaciers gouged the first scar in the earth's surface — torrential rainfall and tremendous floods scoured away billions of cubic feet of earth as the canyon was deepened over the centuries. Today we call the resulting crack in the earth's surface the Deschutes Canyon. The spires were formed by the circular, whirlpool-like action of the immense back-eddies which once formed through this section as primitive floods drained out into the Columbia. The centers of the back-eddies had the least erosive action, and the result was vertical, finger-like rock structures which can still be seen today. Further erosion by freezing moisture, dryness and wind has modified the shapes to their present forms.

*CHECKPOINT
No. 8
85.3

HARRIS CANYON — The canyon opens on the east bank. An old railroad water tower still stands. This area has a rich heritage — the canyon was named for John E. Harris, who homesteaded several hundred yards downstream on the east bank. In the early 1900's Frank Barton owned the homestead, and his caretaker, Jesse Philson, built a complex irrigation system which relied upon a large, wooden waterwheel to lift water from the river and transfer it to wooden flumes for distribution to the entire homestead. Philson's daughter Avis recalls: "We had many teamsters come through from Moro to Tygh Valley and points beyond. Mother would prepare meals for the men, Dad would put the horses in the barns; then early the next morning they would be on their way again. It was like a wayside inn at our place. Our long table, in the dining room, was full many a time. When the railroad was being surveyed and put in across the river, the whole group tented on our island, and rowed across to work each day. They seemed to have an endless supply of good food. Many times after a big meal, the cook would give my Daddy any of a roast that was left. He said the men didn't like leftovers or warmed up food. These leftovers were great treats for us." Today, the property is owned by Ed Sharp of The Dalles. Ed reports that his family has found many Indian artifacts in the Harris Canyon area, including a dried salmon storehouse. Layers of dried salmon were stacked between layers of woven grass mats. This supply gave the Indians sustenance over the winter months and when there were no fish in the river. Petroglyphs are visible a short distance up the canyon, not far from an ancient Indian burial ground.

By the Spring of 1910, both railroads had completed their grades and were ready to lay steel in the Harris Canyon area.

This water wheel was used to irrigate the homestead at Harris Canyon. Note its builder, Jesse Philson, standing on the wheel.

The last remaining water tower stands sentinel at the mouth of Harris Canyon.

Rapid No.	Mileage	Class	

178   85.4   1+   IDENTIFICATION: Harris Island splits the river. Take left channel.

HOW TO: Pull to within 30 feet of the left bank and enter the V-slick to pass through the center, thereby avoiding a shelf of bedrock which extends across the entire channel.

COMMENTS: *Now you are adjacent to the old Harris homestead. The canyon walls open and the river passes along the left side.*

179   85.8   2   IDENTIFICATION: Harris land still on right side (island is approximately 1/2 mile in length); river shallows on left.

HOW TO: Position within 30 feet of the right bank for the first 100 yards. At about midrapids, move to the center to avoid rock outcroppings from right bank. Once in midstream, pass out of rapids on crests of medium standing waves.

COMMENTS: *Campsite on left bank, about 250 yards below No. 179.*

180   86.7   1   IDENTIFICATION: River shallows to form minor whitecaps.

HOW TO: Pass through in midstream and follow standing whitecaps out of riffle.

COMMENTS: *Fall Canyon opens on west bank. Two campsites on west bank. An interesting road which ends abruptly is on the west canyon slope.*

181   87.3   1   IDENTIFICATION: River shallows on left side.

HOW TO: Follow mainstream as it swings to the right bank. Pass within 40 feet of the right bank on the crests of minor standing chop.

COMMENTS: *The remnants of a rock roadbed can be seen on the right bank, approximately 150 yards below No. 181. This old roadbed continues downstream, within a few feet of the river's edge. This was the original road between The Dalles and Moro. Travelers crossed the Deschutes via the Free Bridge (which is 2.6 miles ahead). The road was built by John E. Harris before the turn of the century, and was known as the finest toll road in this area.*

182   88.0   1   IDENTIFICATION: Burn Canyon opens on the west bank; river shallows across its entire width.

HOW TO: Pass through in midstream, riding the small chop.

COMMENTS: *The red color of the lava on the east bank results from increased oxidation because of either age or extensive weathering. A campsite is located on the west bank. Fires are common in this area. In the early days of the railroad, sparks from the engines and brakes would ignite the tinder-dry grasses on both sides of the tracks. Section crews were responsible for extinguishing them before they caused damage. Ted Lewis, track inspector for the Oregon Trunk, recalls chasing many of these fires up the canyon slopes. "Once the fire got started uphill, it could outrun a man on horseback. They were uncontrollable until they reached the top or some level spot," Ted recalls. Strong winds blowing up the canyon fan the blazes and add to the hazards of trying to bring them under control.*

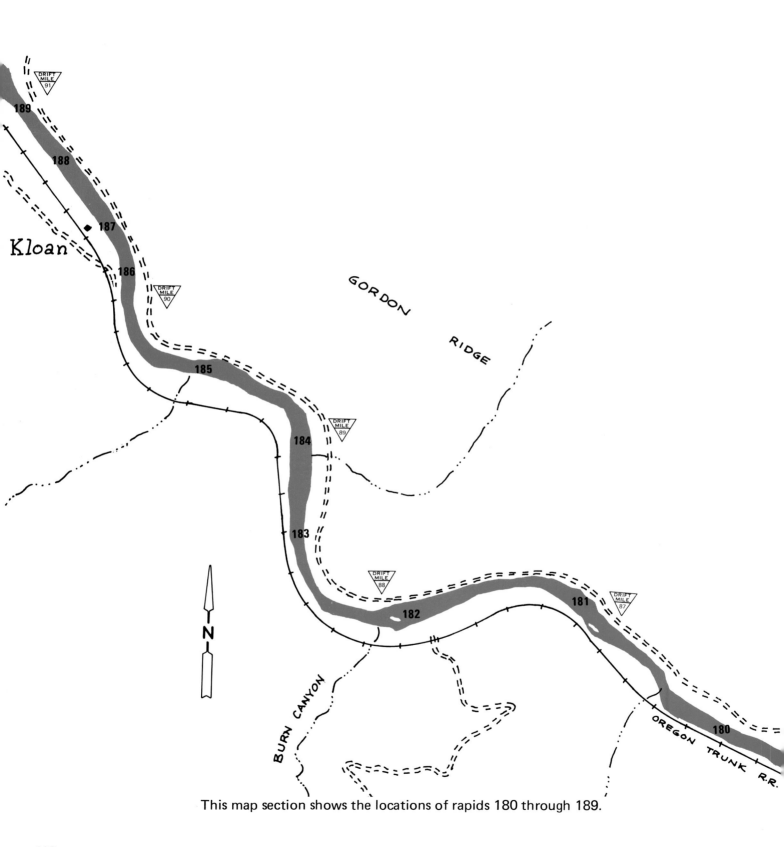

This map section shows the locations of rapids 180 through 189.

183　88.3　1　IDENTIFICATION: Located approximately 200 yards below No. 182; river shallows on right; rocky outcroppings create standing waves on left.

HOW TO: Position in right center, just off standing wave. Ride through center of whitewater.

184　89.0　2　IDENTIFICATION: River shallows and minor whitecaps form across entire river width. This choppy riffle continues for approximately 250 yards; river bends to the left.

HOW TO: Position about 50 feet off the right bank. Watch for submerged boulders on the right half as river flows around the bend to left. Avoid large standing waves created by submerged boulders by moving to midstream and maneuvering to avoid obstructions on both sides.

185　89.6　2　IDENTIFICATION: Power line crosses river overhead; Stecker Canyon opens on west bank; river becomes choppy as it shallows and flows over submerged boulders.

HOW TO: Remain midstream for the first 75 yards, then move to within 30 feet of the left bank to avoid gravel bar extending into river from right. Pass to the right of the largest standing waves on the last 100 yards of the rapids to avoid submerged boulders.

Comments: Campsite on left bank, approximately 100 yards below No. 185.

*CHECKPOINT
NO. 9
90.0*

IDENTIFICATION: FREEBRIDGE — One of the main drawbacks for settlers of Oregon's central plateaus was a lack of adequate transportation and access roads. In 1873, John E. Harris was the first white man to build a functional toll bridge at this site. In 1887, Wasco County purchased the bridge from Harris and changed it to a free bridge. In 1905, the original wooden structure was replaced by a steel and concrete span, which was 150 feet in length and cleared the river by 20 feet. Its cost was $18,000. In 1914, first reports indicated that an unusually forceful gust of wind had blown the bridge down. However, John Petersen discovered dynamite wires attached to its structure as he helped dismantle the fallen span. At that time, there was a second bridge across the Deschutes at Moody, several miles downstream. The Moody bridge was a toll bridge, and some suspect the free bridge destruction was caused by other than a gust of wind. The road approaching the bridge from the west bank was very steep and dangerous, making this route less popular than the easier routes across the river at Sherars Falls and Moody. The first automobile to cross to the east side of the river used this span in 1906. The automobile was a two-cycle Holsman, which was air-cooled and tiller-steered. It was purchased by the Deschutes Telephone Company to substitute for the usual horse-and-buggy. The car was picked up in The Dalles and driven by H. C. Ellis to Bend via the somewhat unreliable road system which existed in this area in those days. The high centered roads were deeply rutted and strewn with rocks, making automobile passage impractical. The Holsman navigated its way over and past stumps, juniper, rocks and hair-raising curves, up and down cliffs and canyons, to reach Bend. Its fenders were ripped, dented scraps of torn metal and were abandoned along the roadside. It can still be seen in Bend at gatherings of the Deschutes Pioneers' Association. By 1910, thousands of unemployed Italian workers crossed this bridge on foot, heading for the construction camps of the two competing railroads which were involved in the last great railroad construction race in the country. Activities were at their peak during those years as the dust-filled roads were jammed with freight wagons, pedestrians, hacks, buggies, men on horseback and an occasional automobile.

The Freebridge as it looked in 1911.

Rapid No.	Mileage	Class	
186	90.0	1	IDENTIFICATION: Two iron bridge piers on right bank; pier in river; whitewater forms as ledges and boulders extend out from left bank. **HOW TO: Position approximately 50 feet from right bank and maneuver as required.**
—	90.1	—	*COMMENTS: "Kloan" is the Chinook jargon word for the number "three." A railroad station on the west bank was named Kloan, because it was the third station from the north end of the Oregon Trunk line. Ted Lewis remembers a head-on collision between two steam engines, just south of Kloan.*
187	90.2	1	IDENTIFICATION: River shallows to form minor whitecaps, approximately 200 yards below No. 187. **HOW TO: Remain midstream and maneuver to avoid rocky outcroppings.** *COMMENTS: Campsite on left.*
188	90.7	1	IDENTIFICATION: Gentle riffle develops. **HOW TO: Pass through in midstream.**
189	90.9	1	IDENTIFICATION: Located approximately 100 yards downstream from No. 188; minor whitecaps cover the width of the river. **HOW TO: Pass through in midstream.**

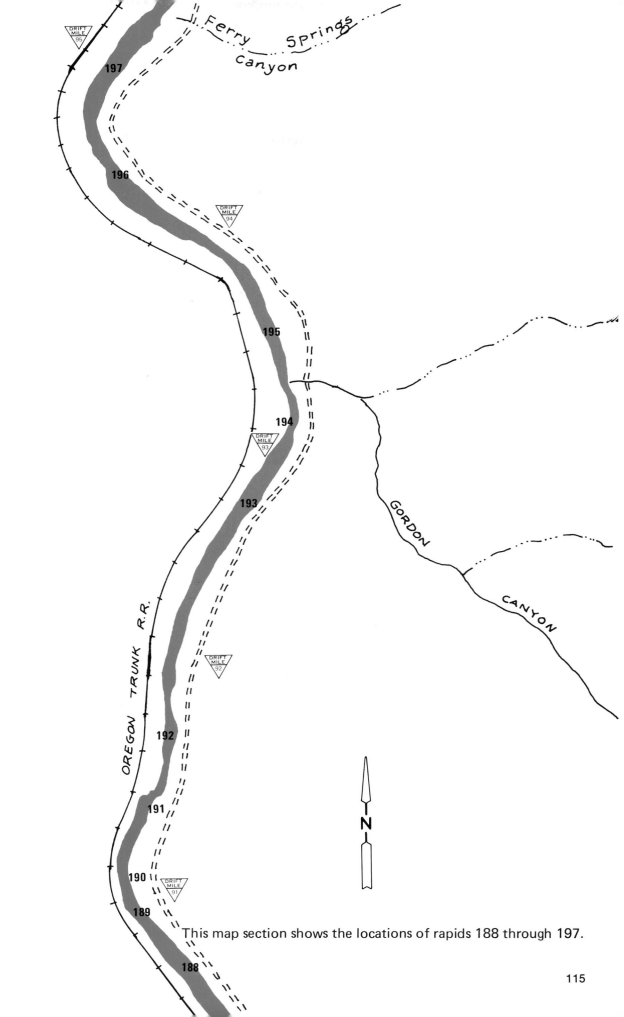

DRIFT
MILE
95

197

196

DRIFT
MILE
94

Ferry Springs
Canyon

195

194

DRIFT
MILE
93

193

GORDON

192

OREGON TRUNK R.R.

DRIFT
MILE
92

CANYON

191

190

DRIFT
MILE
91

N

189

This map section shows the locations of rapids 188 through 197.

188

Gordon Rapids is formed by highly resistant columnar basalt.

Rapid No.	Mileage	Class	
190	91.1	1	IDENTIFICATION: Julia Riffle — Power lines can be seen ahead overhead; river shallows on right.

HOW TO: Pass down midchannel. Avoid rocky outcroppings at lower end by remaining slightly right of midstream. |
| 191 | 91.3 | 1+ | IDENTIFICATION: Power lines are directly overhead.

HOW TO: Enter main chute approximately 50 feet from right bank. Follow mainstream across riverbed. |
| 192 | 91.7 | 2+ | ***SCOUTING MANDATORY***SCOUT FROM RIGHT BANK***

IDENTIFICATION: GORDON RIDGE RAPIDS — Power lines over No. 191 are an upstream warning; water slows to pool on the upstream side of the rapids. A pleasant, sandy beach on the right permits a comfortable pull-out for your scout.

HOW TO: STAGE ONE — Enter by positioning and staying within 10 feet of the right bank. Look ahead 100 feet to prepare for the more difficult Stage Two.

HOW TO: STAGE TWO — Water drops about 6 feet over a highly resistant basalt ledge. Columnar basalt is evident in midriver. Ride through on center of main V-slick, avoiding rock outcroppings on both sides. Look ahead 200 yards to prepare for Stage Three.

HOW TO: STAGE THREE — Pass through on the main V-slot of the right channel. Look ahead 400 yards to prepare for Stage Four. |

HOW TO: STAGE FOUR — Position slightly right of midstream at the entry, then move to right channel to pass within a couple of feet (on the right hand side) of the midstream outcroppings. Follow the main V-slot through a narrow channel at the bottom and exit on small choppy waves for several hundred yards.

Rapid No.	Mileage	Class
193	92.8	1

IDENTIFICATION: Whitewater marks shallowing of the river.

HOW TO: Pass through in midstream.

Courtesy of Mel Olmstead

This picture was taken in 1930. This was one of the last teams of mules to pull a combine in this area. Note that this picture shows two rivers, three counties, two states and two railroads.

194   93.1   3   ***SCOUTING RECOMMENDED***SCOUT FROM RIGHT BANK***

IDENTIFICATION: COLORADO RAPIDS — Also called Grasshopper Rapids and Trestle Rapids. Two railroad trestles are visible in the distance; Gordon Canyon opens ahead on the east bank.

HOW TO: Enter about 50 feet off the right bank; watch for submerged boulders. Pass through on the right side of the main V-slick, about 40 feet from the right bank. Avoid large standing wave and its huge suckhole on the left side, which will overturn all boats and most rafts. Ride out on medium standing waves.

COMMENTS: Gordon Canyon was named after a Scottish homesteader. In 1863, William Nix built a bridge across the Deschutes in this section of the river. This bridge permitted a bypass for the Graham Miller bridge which was located on the Oregon Trail, near the mouth of the river. In 1868, The Dalles Military Road Company purchased the bridge and access roads, but they did not maintain them and high water in 1870 swept the bridge away. Today, only sketchy accounts remain. The old wooden railroad trestle crossing Gordon Canyon became impassable in 1935 after the Deschutes Railroad pulled the rails.

195   93.5   2   IDENTIFICATION: Madden Riffle — River shallows with numerous submerged boulders for several hundred yards, no significant whitewater.

HOW TO: This long stretch can be taken by looking ahead and maneuvering as necessary to avoid the boulders.

This trestle, once located near Colorado Rapids, was destroyed by a grass fire.

Colorado Rapids has a huge suckhole that is capable of overturning any boat.

— 94.0 —

COMMENTS: The river is divided by numerous grass-tufted rocks which form narrow channels. This marks the last identifying feature on the river before Rattlesnake Rapids, which lies just ahead. Look forward to the bend in the river and identify the whitewater splashes which mark Rattlesnake. Move to the left bank to scout. The river shallows severely on the left, and most boats cannot reach the bank, so it is necessary to walk and wade some distance to reach the left bank.

196 94.3 4

IDENTIFICATION: RATTLESNAKE RAPIDS — Also called Posthole Rapids, Wagenblast Rapids and Fence Line Hole. Large churning rapids are visible ahead. Entry appears wide and smooth, but river drops out of sight. Several drownings have occurred at these rapids. A rock ledge extends across the river from the right bank, leaving only a narrow channel on the left side.

HOW TO: Approach left of center. Align with midstream tuft of grass. Pass just to the right side of this tuft. Be careful not to get too far left because of submerged rocks and tricky currents. Once past the tuft, follow the main V-slick which angles slightly left. Be very careful not to let the current push you to the right side (toward the major whitewater) because of a submerged boulder which creates a giant suckhole. The entire force of the Deschutes river is concentrated in this suckhole which must be avoided by passing within 8 feet on its left side. Don't get too far away from it or you will lose control in the shallow water on the left bank. Once past the suckhole, watch for large boulders which protrude in low water for the remainder of the rapids.

COMMENTS: A natural bridge has been eroded from the basalt cliffs on the east bank, approximately 100 yards below No. 196.

197 95.0 1

IDENTIFICATION: Located approximately 200 yards below No. 196; bedrock in midstream splits river; both the center V-slick and the right channel are passable.

HOW TO: Pass through with no trouble.

198 95.2 1

IDENTIFICATION: Ferry Springs Canyon opens on the east bank; minor whitecaps cross the river.

HOW TO: Pass through in midstream and avoid standing waves (which hide submerged boulders).

— 95.9 —

COMMENTS: A cable crosses the river overhead. It serves as a trolley crossing to the Moody gauging station. There was once a town of Moody, with a post office and all the niceties. However, when the railroad was completed, the population moved away, the post office closed and only a section headquarters for track maintenance remains. Moody was named after Malcolm A. Moody of The Dalles, a member of a local pioneer family and a U.S. Representative in the Congress. He also owned a power site near the mouth of the Deschutes. The Oregon Trunk had to ferry supplies and equipment from the Great Northern tracks on the north side of the Columbia. They used the old sternwheeler **Norma**, *which was built in 1869 by Jacob Kamm, in Huntington, Oregon. To reach this part of the state, the 488 ton, 168 foot sternwheeler was navigated through Hells Canyon, shooting the rapids and falls. For a number of years, she was used to transport wheat to Lewiston, Idaho. During the railroad construction era,* **Norma** *ferried rails, ties and building materials to the yard*

at Moody. Upon completion of the Oregon Trunk railroad, she ferried passengers from trains which unloaded on the north bank of the Columbia River. Before the completion of Fall Bridge over Celilo Falls, she powered barges which transported entire trains across the Columbia. Moody was the main supply base for the construction camps which worked up the Deschutes canyon. The uniformity of discharge of the river is remarkably constant; the lowest flow on record at the Moody gauging station is 3,380 cubic feet per second recorded on September 16-19, 1931.

Rapid No.	Mileage	Class
199	96.0	2

IDENTIFICATION: Moody Rapids — Identify by Moody gauging station upstream and power lines overhead at entry.

HOW TO: At entry, pass down midstream, avoiding boulders as necessary. At lower end, avoid midstream ledges by moving to the right bank and passing out of the final several hundred feet of whitewater. The calm water which you enter is The Dalles Dam pool.

—	96.6	—

There is an easy take-out on the west bank, several hundred yards upstream from the Interstate 80 Freeway bridge.

Aerial view of the Deschutes River as it empties into The Dalles Dam pool.

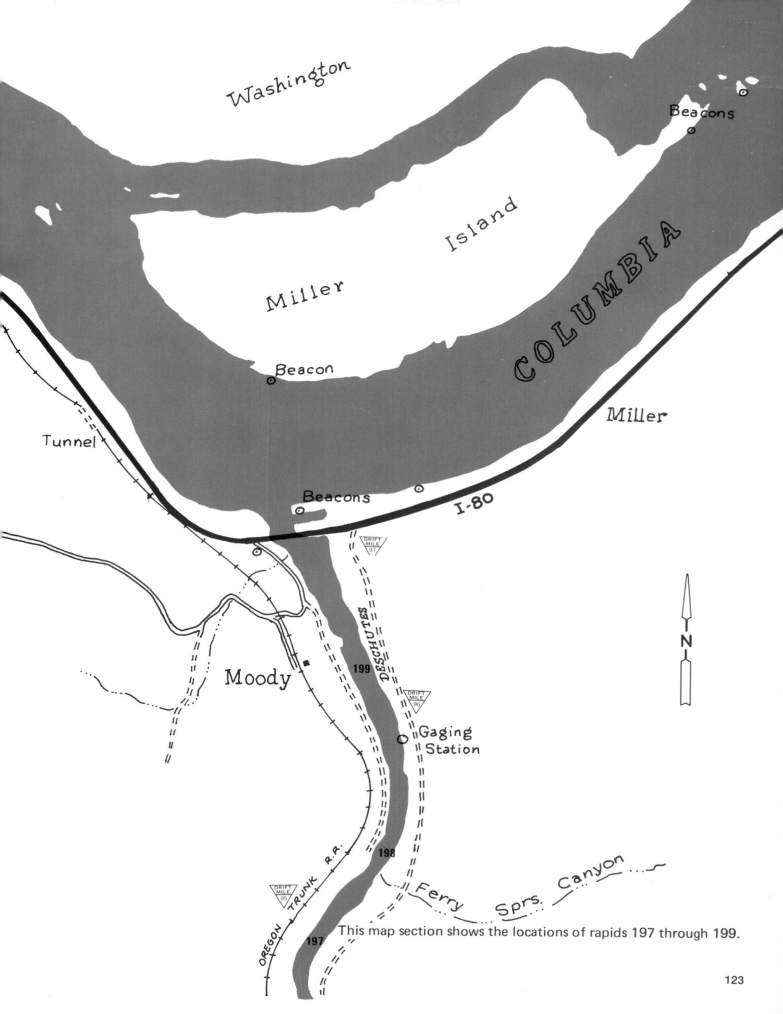

Washington

Miller Island

COLUMBIA

Beacons

Beacon

Tunnel

Miller

Beacons

I-80

DRIFT MILE 97

DESCHUTES

199

DRIFT MILE 96

Moody

Gaging Station

N

198

DRIFT MILE 95

OREGON TRUNK R.R.

Ferry Sprs. Canyon

197

This map section shows the locations of rapids 197 through 199.

Everyone works at camp. Let's make sure that these kids have free flowing rivers to float down when they grow up.

INTRODUCTION TO HAZARDS

There are a few important hazards that are worth noting along the river. It is a good idea to make sure that everyone in your party is aware of these potential dangers. By understanding and knowing where to look for these hazards, it is possible to avoid serious problems.

BLACK WIDOW SPIDER

The species found along the Deschutes river is particularly venomous. The female is approximately 1/2 inch in length, with a shiny velvety-black back. When turned over, she displays a small red hourglass mark on an almost rounded abdomen. Other names for this spider are, shoe-button spider, red mark, red back and hourglass spider. The male is much smaller than the female and is eaten by the female once fertilization is complete, giving her the strange name.

Cool, dark places are preferred by the Black Widow, so be careful when moving rocks and wood. Our only contacts with this spider along the Deschutes have been when gathering wood for bonfires.

55 deaths in the United States have been attributed to Black Widow spiders, whose venom is usually painful but not fatal. However, the non-fatal symptoms are very unpleasant because the venom is a neurotoxin which affects the nervous system to cause severe pain, muscular cramps, paralysis and hypertension.

This arachnid is shy and will defend itself only if there is no escape. The male is considered harmless because it cannot carry enough venom to seriously affect humans.

POISON OAK

Habit: erect shrubs 3 to 10 feet in height, or tree-climbing vines with shiny, dark green leaves which turn varying shades of red and yellow in the fall. *Leaves:* alternate, 3 ovate-shaped leaflets. The terminal leaflet is larger than the 2 lateral leaflets. Surfaces are smooth and shiny. *Flowers:* small, long-stemmed, inconspicuous, yellowish green, borne in loose, pendulous clusters. *Fruit:* round to globular, grayish white, striated, persist after the

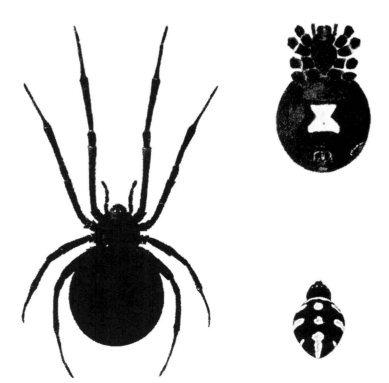

Black Widow.

SHINY LEAVES

Poison Oak.

leaves have fallen. *Remarks:* occurs on many of the slopes along the Deschutes. Camping sites usually have some examples of poison oak nearby.

Poison oak is toxic to most individuals, immunity is relative. Individuals who have not been bothered by poison oak for some years may find themselves suddenly sensitive. Fumes from the burning plants are especially toxic, causing respiratory reactions which may be extremely critical. Don't burn it in your camp's bonfires. Bees are attracted to the flowers in the spring, but none of the toxicity of the plant is transmitted through the nectar. Horses and cattle can browse the species with immunity. Household pets that wander through the plant are carriers of the irritating resins and can transmit the poisonous substance to owners who handle them.

RATTLESNAKE

These are heavily-bodied, highly venomous snakes. When disturbed, the rattler vibrates his tail (and rattle) as if giving warning that he is about to strike. The rattle consists of a number of loosely interlocked shells, each of which was the scale originally covering the tip of the tail. The end scales wear out from use, so there can be a different number of segments in the rattles of two rattlers of the same age. In the wilds, these rattles seldom

Note the two fangs of the Western Rattle-snake.

This "rattler" is ready to strike.

exceed 14 in number. The most effective number is 8, larger rattles resulting in muted sounds.

Unless provoked, the rattler of the Deschutes river canyon will make no attempt to strike. This is unlike the Western Diamondback Rattler, which may pursue an intruder. A snake's poisonousness depends upon its age (the younger it is, the smaller the volume of venom it will carry), its natural range (snakes of the same species from one part of a range may be more venomous than those from another part of the same range), and the time elapsed since the last strike made by the snake. Once depleted, the venom may take as long as 2 months to regenerate completely.

The main food of the rattlesnake is small warm-blooded animals, such as mice, chipmunks and other small rodents. Young rattlesnakes feed mainly on cold-blooded animals such as frogs, salamanders and lizards. A rattlesnake requires only 1/10 as much water as other mammals of comparable size and weight because its skin is almost perfectly waterproof.

All rattlesnakes give birth to live young. Mating is in the spring, and the litter may vary from 1 to 60 baby snakes, depending upon the size of the mother (the usual number is from 10 to 20). Few baby rattlesnakes survive their first year because of the high toll taken by predators and enemies, such as hawks, skunks, snake-eating snakes, pigs, deer and other hoofed animals.

Watch for rattlesnakes during the heat of the day, at which time they will be located in the shade of rocks, trees and plants. A very popular place for them is lying next to green grass turf hummocks. In the evenings and early mornings they will come out in the open to sun themselves on the sand and open rocks. Expect to see rattlesnakes anywhere along your journey down the Deschutes. Be prepared, carry a snake-bite kit and be familiar with its correct use.

SCORPION

In the United States, it has been estimated that more people are killed annually by scorpions than by snakes. Scorpions are notorious for their stings, the venom of which is sometimes fatal to man. They range in length from 1/4 inch to as much as 8 inches. The species found along the Deschutes river seldom exceeds 2 inches. The body is segmented and the head bears a pair of pincer-like claws, similar to the lobster. The thorax has 4 segments, each with a pair of walking legs. The abdomen has 6

Scorpions.

segments, tapering to a single sharp stinger at the end with a small opening supplied by two relatively large venom glands.

Scorpions hunt by night, the prey consisting entirely of insects and spiders. They seize the victim with their large claws and tear it to pieces, extracting its body juices. The scorpion will sting its victim only if resistance is offered. The prey is slowly eaten, an hour or more being spent to consume a single beetle.

Scorpions can survive long periods of time without eating, and they never drink. They receive their moisture from their food, like most other desert-dwelling animals.

Scorpions perform a mating courtship, at which time the female is grasped by the male, who pushes her to a suitable location where he scrapes away the soil with his feet and deposits his spermatophore. Then, still holding the female by her claws, he maneuvers her over the spermatophore so she can sorb it into her body. The young scorpions are born alive, one or two at a time, over a period of several weeks. At birth, the baby scorpions ride around on the mother's back. Only after their first molt do they leave the mother and become independent. They may live to an age of 5 years. Look for them under the rocks away from the river's edge.

WATER HEMLOCK

Habit: perennial; several erect stems from 2 to 5 feet tall; 1 to 5 tuberous rootstalks which are 1 to 3 inches in length and 1/2 inch in width; a sagittal (lengthwise) section reveals the horizontal chamber structure of the rootstalks; when the main stalk is cut, an oily, amber liquid is emitted which is extremely toxic. *Leaves:* compound; leaflets from 2 to 4 inches in length, with 2 serrated margins. Primary lateral veins of each leaflet are located in the depressed grooves of the leaflet. *Flowers:* small, white, flat-topped clusters. Each cluster is 2 to 5 inches in diameter. Blossoms show from June to August. *Fruit:* fruit-pod is 1/8 inch in length. Pods are evident in the months of August through October. *Remarks:* this is one of the most poisonous plants in the west. The entire plant can cause death, with the roots being most toxic.

There have been several cases of the plant causing deaths due to browsing cattle eating it along the riverbanks. Several years ago, an experienced naturalist mistook this plant for wild celery and died within hours of picking it from the river's edge.

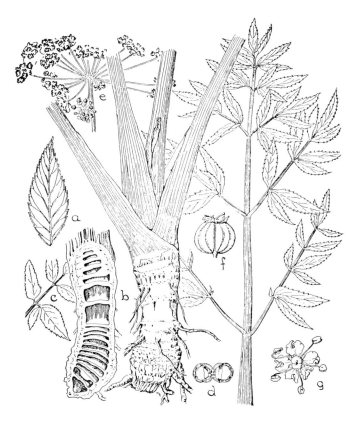

Water Hemlock.

You can find Water Hemlock anywhere along the river, with good examples of it showing at White-horse Rapids and along the lower river stretch.

INTRODUCTION TO MAMMALS

As you drift down the canyon you may see many interesting animals along the river's edge. The mammals which follow can be observed as they prowl along the slopes and ridges of the Deschutes canyon.

BEAVER

This member of the rodent family may grow to the extreme size of 100 pounds, but normally ranges from 40 to 50 pounds in weight and 3 to 5 feet in length. Its major characteristic is its broad, flattened tail which it slaps on the water surface as it dives. The resulting loud crack may serve as a defensive action, startling its attacker and biologists also believe it gives warning to other beavers in the area.

History shows that the beaver pelt has been one of the world's most popular choices for fur garments. Locally, the Hudson's Bay Fur Company at Vancouver, Washington, recorded purchasing a total of 405,472 beaver pelts in the years between 1834

The Beaver is Oregon's State Animal.

and 1837. By 1893, the beaver population was almost totally decimated and the animal was near extinction in Oregon. Laws were passed to protect the animal, and in 1951 trapping of beavers was allowed again.

The beaver's abilities have contributed to its reputation of possessing high intelligence. It is known that beavers are capable of constructing complicated dams which will hold back millions of gallons of water; they have been observed as they construct intricate canals and waterways to float their trees from the felling site to their dams and lodges, and many observers believe that beavers deliberately notch trees in such a way that they work with wind direction to control the final positioning of the fallen tree.

Litters of 3 or 4 are produced in the spring, and the social nature of the animal results in large populations developing rapidly in their area. A beaver mound is always constructed on small streams, rather than on swiftly flowing or higher volume rivers. On the Deschutes river you may see beaver, but you will not see a dam or construction project.

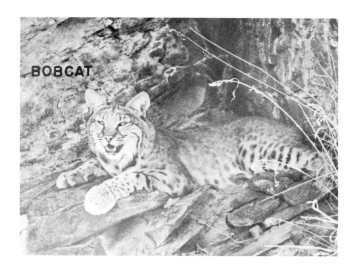

Mountain Lion.

BOBCAT

The bobcat is named because of its short bobtail, a characteristic which it shares with its cousin, the lynx. Bobcats are yellowish brown in color, with dark spots on most of the body. Total length is about 3 feet, and height at the shoulder is 14 to 16 inches. Weight of a bobcat varies from 20 to 30 pounds. To avoid confusion with the lynx, look at the ears which have shorter ear tufts and the tail which has a white tip instead of a black tip.

Bobcats are predators of small birds and mammals, domestic livestock and small sheep. Their diet consists of large quantities of rodents and they wage war on domestic house-cats that have gone wild. Generally, normal trapping pressures keep bobcat numbers under control, but in some areas trappers are employed and bounties are paid as an inducement to hunters.

An average litter of 3 is born in the spring. Its nocturnal habits make this animal difficult to observe.

COUGAR

This largest member of the cat family found in Oregon is only rarely seen in this area. Cougars prefer timbered areas and seldom venture into the open. Other names for the cougar are mountain lion and panther. When cornered, the cougar is a match for the best of dogs. Man is his only effective enemy.

The cougar in Oregon varies in color from yellowish brown to dark reddish brown, depending upon the area in which he lives. The distinguishing feature is the cougar's long body and tail, resulting in animal lengths of 8½ feet or more. The cougar is the only large, long-tailed cat in Oregon.

Despite reports to the contrary, cougars seldom attack humans and make every effort to avoid a confrontation. Cougars become nuisances when they develop a taste for domestic cattle and horses, but they usually avoid civilization altogether.

Cougars do not hibernate, therefore they must hunt for food all year. Deer are the animals most often killed and eaten. Rabbits and porcupine, elk, raccoons, skunks, antelope and domestic animals are also eaten by the cougar.

Young cougar may be born at any time during the year, and the average litter numbers two.

COYOTE

Whereas his larger relative, the wolf, has failed to adapt to civilization, the coyote has succeeded remarkably well, and the Deschutes canyon has a

COYOTE

MULE DEER

Mule deer are commonly seen along the banks of the Deschutes, particularly in early morning and at dusk. Although similar in appearance to the Black-Tailed deer, the "muley" has much larger ears. It also possesses a rope-like white tail with a black tip, surrounded by a light colored rump patch. The deer's summer coat is reddish-brown, with lighter colored underparts. Males may weigh up to 250 pounds, females are smaller.

Fawns are born in May and June, and twins are common. The doe and her fawns stay together until the following spring, when the family separates. In the winter months you will see these deer herding together as they move from one grazing area to another along the slopes on both banks of the river. The major browse is sagebrush, mountain mahogany and bitterbrush.

Antlers of the male are a bony growth which develops from the front of the skull each year. The antlers are first covered with a hairy skin called "velvet," and when the growth stops, the skin dries out and sloughs off, leaving an exposed bony structure. As the deer matures, the number of "forks" increases. The horns are used in mating rituals, and are shed when the mating season is done.

number of coyote. Often a coyote is mistaken for a wolf, however the smaller size of the coyote is a reliable identifying characteristic. The coyote averages about 30 pounds, or one-third the weight of the wolf. Body length averages 4 feet, and height at the shoulders is 12 to 18 inches.

The coyote is widely distributed and is known as the most destructive mammal of prey in the state. In some cases, the coyote's eating habits are a nuisance, particularly when he takes domestic stock. In other cases, the coyote is considered a control factor, particularly on the rabbit and rodent population. Consequently, if the coyote is too heavily hunted the rabbit and rodent population increases.

Coyote pups are born in April and May. The average litter numbers 7. Coyotes have crossed with domestic dogs and the offspring may be a large, vicious animal. Some of these crossed breeds are mistaken for wolves.

As you journey down the Deschutes you may see coyotes at any time, but they are more evident in the morning or late evening, as they come near the river to drink. The coyote is the songster of the canyon and you may be awakened some evening by his lonesome tones.

Mule Deer.

MINK

As you drift the Deschutes you may catch glimpses of these small animals darting back and forth along the river's edge. Males are from 20 to 30 inches in length, females being about half this size. The color of a wild mink ranges from light to dark brown, with an identifying white patch on the lower lip.

Mink are aggressive hunters, both on land and in the water. They kill not only for food, but also for sport. Their nocturnal nature makes them more active in the evening hours. Their food consists largely of fish, frogs, crayfish and ducks. Because they kill more than they eat, their dens usually contain considerable stores of excess food.

During mating season, the mink makes a curious purring sound, but remains noiseless during the rest of the year. There are 5 or 6 kits born in the fur-and-feather nest, and the family stays together from spring to autumn. Young mink strike out on their own after 6 months of age, establishing a new private territory nearby.

Mink possess musk glands which produce a scent as obnoxious as that of a skunk. Perhaps this is the reason so few animals choose to challenge the mink.

Muskrat.

Mink.

MUSKRAT

You may see this fur-bearing mammal swimming near the rushes and reeds in slow back eddies. The Deschutes river basin is one of Oregon's muskrat strongholds.

Muskrats burrow underwater entries to their dens in the river bank for protection. Like his cousin, the beaver, a muskrat's pelt value depends upon the color of his coat; the darker the coat color, the more valuable the pelt. Even in appearance, the muskrat resembles a small beaver. However, the tail is different — the tail of a beaver is broad and flattened horizontally, the tail of a muskrat is narrow and flattened vertically.

The average size of a muskrat is 17 to 25 inches in length, with a shoulder height of 4 to 5 inches. Its fur is dense, with soft gray underfur covered by long, dark guard hairs.

A litter of 4 to 6 is born underground in the spring. The muskrat is a social creature and large numbers can accumulate in the area of the parents.

There are mixed feelings about the muskrat. In some places the animal is considered a pest because of its odor and tunnel-boring activities. In other areas, the animal is imported deliberately to control marshes and weeds which threaten to block waterways and channels. The muskrat feeds on the soft lower parts of water plants.

Two glands at the base of the tail secrete a powerful musk odor which gives the animal its name.

OTTER

One of the clowns of the animal world is the otter. For displaying sheer enjoyment of living and delight in its environment, this frivolous animal takes the prize. Some of its activities include follow the leader, tag and sliding down mud or snow-covered slopes into the water. His impishness makes him a disgusting pest to the hardworking beaver trying to build a dam.

Otter travel by water whenever possible. Their short legs and webbed feet make them excellent swimmers, but rather poor "landlubbers." When crossing land they travel with long, loping jumps. If forced to, they can outrun a man for a short distance.

Otter fur is one of the finest furs available, because of its dark color and density. It is equalled only by the fur of its cousin, the sea otter. Color of both sexes is a rich dark brown, with the underparts, throat and muzzle often a grayish color.

An otter may be mistaken for a weasel, however it is generally larger than a weasel if it is mature. Otter range from 3½ to 4½ feet in length and measure 9 to 10 inches at the shoulder. Weight ranges from 10 to 25 pounds, with females being smaller.

Normally, 2 or 3 otter pups are born in April in a bank burrow or in abandoned beaver or muskrat dens. The family stays and plays together until fall.

The diet of an otter consists of shellfish, fish and other animals. Their reduced numbers make them interesting rather than annoying, except in certain specific instances. Otter may be seen anywhere along the shore, but they are most likely to be seen near the back-eddies.

RACCOON

The masked prowler of the night is an apt name for the raccoon. One of the most distinguished characteristics of this friendly rover is his black mask. This, coupled with a ringed tail, makes the raccoon easy to identify.

Raccoons are from 10 to 16 inches tall at the shoulder, and weigh from 10 to 25 pounds. Some large specimens have reached weights of 50 pounds. The color is grayish-black, with a prominent black mask and ringed tail.

Otter.

Raccoon

The raccoon is a nocturnal wanderer, but can often be seen along the banks of the river in the early morning and just before dusk. Night raids on chicken houses and forays into corn patches are not uncommon once a taste for such pleasures has been acquired by an occasional "coon." When he eats, the raccoon washes or dunks his food in water before eating it. This characteristic makes him appear almost human and endears him to wild animal observers. When food becomes scarce during the winter, the raccoon often curls up for long periods of sleep, though this is not true hibernation as with ground squirrels and marmots. At times, several raccoon families will share the same den.

Young raccoons are born in April or May, with the average litter numbering four or five.

INTRODUCTION TO BIRDS

The river supports a wide variety of bird life. Drifting down the canyon, the interested observer may identify many species of birds. Many migratory birds nest in this area. They can range in size from the smallest swallow to the mighty bald eagle.

CHUKAR PARTRIDGE

This partridge is a newcomer to the Deschutes river canyon, having been first introduced to central Oregon in the 1950's. It is a native of the middle East and central Asia. The Deschutes stock originated in India.

Chukars thrive in the steep, rocky sagebrush and grassland areas along the riverbank. Some low bushes or shrubs are needed for loafing and escape cover.

The Chukar is somewhat larger than a Hungarian partridge, but smaller than a pheasant. Adult plumage is pale grayish-brown with a bluish cast on the breast. The tan flanks are conspicuously marked with vertical black bars, and black bands extend from the top of the beak backward through the eyes and down the sides of the neck to join on the upper breast.

The loud, raucous calling of the Chukars can be heard echoing in the canyon, particularly during mating season. Although a fine game bird, they are under little hunting pressure at the present time because of their preference for steep and rugged terrain.

GOLDEN EAGLE

This noble bird was so stately that only kings in medieval Europe were permitted to use it for hunting. The female is larger than the male, standing 36 inches tall and with a wingspan up to 8 feet.

The food of the majestic bird ranges from small rodents, snakes, fish and carrion to tortoises and foxes. Golden eagles possess a high level of intelligence which is employed in their hunting techniques and characteristics. They may flush rabbits from cover, and one oldtimer reported a pair of eagles working together as a team to drive a deer over a cliff. In Texas, where the birds were slaughtered from airplanes, several incidents were reported in which eagles attacked and damaged the hunters' airplanes in retaliation. The intelligence and bravery of the eagle has been used by herdsmen who train them to protect their flocks of sheep from marauding wolves.

Eagles mate for life and share a common hunting range which no other adult eagles may enter. Upon the death of either mate, the other will select a new partner during the next breeding season. As a rule, 2 white-and-brown flecked eggs are laid and

Golden Eagle.

incubated by the female for 40 days, with the male occasionally feeding her. When the chicks are hatched, he brings the majority of food to the nest. After 10 weeks the chicks leave the nest and perch on nearby ledges, awaiting their parents' return to feed them. Within a few more weeks the birds are capable of flight.

In flight, this bird is identified by its yellow beak and feet which give it its name. The wings appear broad, with end feathers spread and curved upwards. It soars at great heights and can be seen hovering motionless, or gracefully surveying the canyon below as it patrols its territory near the Deschutes.

KILLDEER

The killdeer commonly breeds along the gravel bars of the Deschutes. It may remain through the winter unless snow or ice forces a retreat to warmer climates.

A medium-sized plover, it is readily distinguished from other shorebirds by the two black bands across a snowy breast and the rufous rump and tail-patch. The name "killdeer" is derived from its distinguished alarm call "kill-dee," which it utters at the first sign of danger and continues until the intruder or danger has passed.

Sea Gull.

GULLS

There are many species of gulls along the Deschutes. Both freshwater and saltwater types intermingle. Some are brown and some are white, depending upon their maturity. Dark brown gulls may be the same species as those which are pure white.

Gulls and man interact to increase the numbers of the birds because of their scavenging nature. Year round food supplies assure a good gull population in the Deschutes canyon.

RED-TAILED HAWK

Few hawks take the abuse that this one does. Usually called the "chicken-hawk," it is the most commonly seen and the most often killed. The red-tailed hawk frequently takes rodents near barnyards and is therefore assumed to be after the chickens. Actually, it has been proven that birds of all types account for less than 12 percent of the food of the red-tail.

The bird's large size, light-colored underparts, black-tipped flight feathers and a dark band across the body help identify the male red-tail in flight. As the name indicates, the upper surface of the tail in the adult is bright brick red and can be seen as

KILLDEER

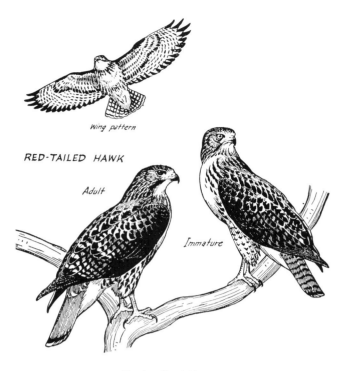

Red-tailed Hawk.

Blue Heron.

the bird wheels, turns or perches.

Body length of the red-tail varies from 19 to 25 inches. The wingspread of the male is from 45 to 51 inches, and the female is larger than the male. Her wingspread is from 50 to 58 inches.

BLUE HERON

The stately blue heron can be seen along the banks of the Deschutes. It is often mistaken for a crane, but can be distinguished by its bluish-gray plumage, white head with black crest, and a dagger-like bill. Individual specimens vary considerably in size, ranging from 40 to 48 inches in length and having wingspreads up to 72 inches. In flight, the heron always flies with recurved neck.

Although the principal food of the blue heron is various kinds of fish, its diet also includes snakes, frogs, mice, salamanders and insects. It fishes by night as well as by day, employing both still-hunting and stalking techniques.

RED-WINGED BLACKBIRD

A vivid red patch on the wing identifies the male of this species. Females are drab brown. This bird can be seen nesting in the willows and alders along the banks of the Deschutes.

Male red-wings are territorial in nature and will challenge any intruder which enters their area of dominance. An interesting study of the bird's territorial behavior can be observed by painting red patches on the side of a stuffed black sock and hanging it on a limb in a red-wing's territory. The bird will attack an "intruder" and attempt to drive it from the area.

The migrating male reaches the Deschutes canyon in March, where it establishes a territory for the female who arrives a few weeks later. In the fall, entire red-wing families congregate to migrate away from the Deschutes canyon.

CLIFF SWALLOW

This small bird can be seen flying over the water near its nest. The nest is a gourdlike "jug" of mud, often built on the face of a vertical cliff or boulder.

The cliff swallow's rusty or buff-colored rump is an identifying feature. In flight, the swallow will glide, ending each glide with a much steeper climb, almost like the action of a "roller-coaster."

WESTERN CANADA GOOSE

Oregon is located within the Pacific Flyway, and one of the more popular birds to use this flyway is the Western Canada Goose. This large "honker" is likely to establish nesting sites wherever grain crops and protected marshes are available.

We have seen large numbers of geese during the winter months along the Deschutes. Some geese live near the river year round, others stop temporarily on their flights to points further south. Since the Deschutes never freezes solid, there is always open water for resting and feeding.

An average size for the Western Canada Goose is 9 to 12 pounds, with some large birds reaching 16 pounds. In flight, the geese assume a typical "V" pattern.

Each goose mates for life. If either partner dies, the survivor does not mate again. The gander is very protective when his mate is on the nest and will defend her from any intruder, including wolves and humans. The female lays from 4 to 10 eggs, the usual number being 5 or 6. After a 28 to 30 day incubation period, the goslings are born and they leave the nest within a few weeks.

During the warmer months, when river traffic is greatest, the geese will browse in the sagebrush at some distance from the river. The Trout Creek area is a good place to watch for this attractive brave bird.

Belted Kingfisher.

BELTED KINGFISHER

The kingfisher may be seen flying with uneven wingbeats, or hovering with rapidly beating wings in anticipation of a plunge to the water's surface.

When the kingfisher is perched on a tree limb, you can observe its big head and large bill. A distinct white band resembles a collar around its neck. The kingfisher is larger than a robin and has a brushy crest on top of its head. In flight, the bird seems to always be cackling or rattling in a non-musical voice.

PIGEONS AND DOVES

In the lower Deschutes you will see numerous flocks of various types of domestic and semi-wild pigeons. Colonies are located on the favorable nesting sites of the cliffs. These birds have escaped captivity and are not native to this area.

A close cousin of the common pigeon is the mourning dove. A delightful experience awaits the river traveler who awakens to the gentle cooing of this stately small bird. Doves may be seen perching or feeding on the ground. When frightened into flight, a distinct whistling sound is created by their rapidly beating wings.

Canadian Geese.

Water Ouzel.

Common Merganser.

WATER OUZEL

This small, slate-colored bird is shaped like a chunky, oversized wren with a stubby tail. Its legs are a pale color and the eyelids are white. When it walks it has a bobbing motion.

The uniqueness of the "dipper" is its ability to submerge beneath the surface of the river when feeding on small animals living in the mosses which are attached to submerged rocks. Some say it actually walks on the bottom.

You may also notice that you will never see two of them together. It is a very independent bird.

WESTERN MEADOWLARK

This attractive bird may be recognized by its yellow breast with a black bib under its throat, and white outer tail feathers. The Western Meadowlark is Oregon's state bird.

Watch for this beautiful bird in open grassy areas along the banks of the Deschutes. Its pretty song can be heard during the spring of the year as it establishes territory during the nesting season. The meadowlark is a migratory bird and first appears in the Deschutes canyon in March.

COMMON MERGANSER

The merganser is a year-round resident of the Deschutes. In flight, mergansers fly in formation, low over the surface of the water.

Males have a dark green head and long white body. Females are gray with a crested light red head. During the summer, the birds can be seen swimming with their young.

Mergansers are one of the stronger swimmers in the duck family. Note that the merganser's bill is modified into a beak for effectiveness in its fish-catching talents.

OSPREY

The osprey is a rare find along the Deschutes nowadays. In some areas of the eastern United States it is protected and provided with artificial nesting sites in attempts to rebuild its numbers.

Osprey feed mainly on fish, with such species as carp and suckers making up a large part of its diet. Often your first sight of an osprey will be as it drops down to the water's surface to take a fish. On occasion osprey will eat other types of food, such as rodents, frogs and birds.

An osprey's wings are long and pointed and the

bird has an over-all white color when viewed from underneath. It has a dark, slate blue back, and the tail is marked with six or seven narrow blackish bands, and is tipped in white. The average wing-spread is 54 to 72 inches, and the body length ranges from 21 to 25 inches. As would be expected, the osprey's feet are large and the toes are arranged with one reversible for better grasping.

Osprey.

INTRODUCTION TO FISH

The Deschutes river is one of the most outstanding trout streams in the Northwest. The river's uniform stream flow and temperature supports a large native populations of rainbow trout. Fishermen from all over the country visit the Deschutes each summer in search of the famous Deschutes "red-sides." These beautiful trout are very strong and provide a good aerial battle when hooked on a fly.

The river also supports a good run of steelhead and salmon. The Deschutes gained great notoriety when a 28 pound world record steelhead was taken on fly-fishing gear.

RAINBOW TROUT

The Deschutes river is famous in the Northwest for its resident rainbow trout. Fishing clubs and associations have been structured around the reputation of the beautiful fighting fish. There is no race of rainbow which can surpass the Deschutes strain for gamefish fighting and eating qualities.

The two species of rainbow found in the Deschutes are the resident rainbow trout and the migratory steelhead. Steelhead are considered in another section of this book. Another common name for the native rainbow is the Deschutes River Redsides. It seldom reaches more than 24 inches in length and 6 pounds in weight.

The best fishing site is in the Whitehorse Rapids section of the river, probably because it is the only area which is inaccessible by road. Fewer trout are caught in the lower Deschutes because spawning beds and water temperatures are not ideal. Artificial lures and flies are readily taken by the rainbow. Its acrobatic characteristics make it a prize catch for all anglers.

Rainbows are bluish-green on the back and silvery on the belly. A generous sprinkling of black spots appear along the back, and on the dorsal, adipose and caudal fins. The beautiful spectrum of colors of a freshly caught rainbow has given it its name. Spawning season usually occurs in the spring.

A small, but beautiful, Deschutes River rainbow trout. Once males get a bit larger than this, and mature, their sides often redden up around spawning time and they frequently are called "red-sides."

WHITEFISH

Oregon's whitefish is related to the trout and char family. It thrives best in clear, cold water.

Trout-like in appearance, the body is silvery in color with a bronze or darkish back. Its mouth is small with weak teeth. The Deschutes whitefish seldom reaches 20 inches in length, and usually weighs less than 3 pounds.

Many anglers consider the whitefish to be a trash fish and throw it away as undesirable, however it has many gamelike qualities. It readily strikes lures and artificial flies and offers a spirited fight, characteristic of other gamefish. Its flesh is firm and palatable.

Spawning occurs in the fall and early winter.

Whitefish.

BROWN TROUT

The brown trout has been successfully introduced to the Deschutes from Europe. The world record brown trout weighed 41 pounds, but in the Deschutes the average weight is less than 8 pounds.

A golden brown color with red and dark gray spots on the body identifies this sportfish. Brown trout have been confused with dolly varden trout, but can be distinguished by the many body spots below the lateral line, many of which have pink or orange edges, resembling colored rings or halos.

A breeding male develops a hooked snout, which sometimes fools the fisherman who thinks he has caught a small salmon. Spawning occurs in the fall, usually from October to January.

Anglers consider the brown trout a great challenge because of its wariness. It is the most difficult to catch.

DOLLY VARDEN

DOLLY VARDEN

This member of the char family lacks the dash and zip of its cousin, the rainbow trout. Fishermen seldom show much enthusiasm for this fish, and most regard it as a cannibal. It has been considered a threat to the salmon population, and in certain areas it has been declared a nuisance and bounties have been offered for its removal from local waters.

The fish received its name from the Dolly Varden fashions of the 1870's, and shares a color combination popular in those days. The fish is an olive green to brownish on the back and sides, cream colored on the belly, and possesses orange and red spots.

The dolly varden reaches weights of 20 pounds or more; the world record is 32 pounds. It readily strikes bait or lures, and it offers a hard, deep-running fight when hooked. It has a pleasant, palatable taste.

STEELHEAD

The steelhead is a sea-run rainbow trout. It is the largest race of rainbow in Oregon. Although some steelhead remain in fresh water their entire lives, the Deschutes steelhead migrates to the ocean and returns after spending two years in salt water. They begin to enter the river in July and average between 6 and 8 pounds.

Spawning occurs in the Deschutes, Bakeoven Creek, Buck Hollow Creek, Trout Creek and the Warm Springs River. Many steelhead travel 100 miles up the Deschutes, where they are trapped for propogation programs.

The Deschutes is an outstanding Northwest steelhead stream and a world record steelhead was caught on a fly just above the mouth of the river in 1946. The elated angler was Morley Griswold, the late governor of Nevada. The 28 pound fish was caught on 5¾-ounce split bamboo fly rod.

Morley Griswold holds his world record Deschutes River steelhead.

A female steelhead may deposit as many as 2,500 eggs. Smaller females lay fewer eggs. The eggs are deposited in nests called "redds," which are 8 to 10 inches deep and of varying width. Redds are dug by the tail and body of the female steelhead. As soon as the eggs are laid, the male "buck" swims slowly over the exposed eggs and deposits a milky fluid called "milt" onto the surface of the nest to fertilize the eggs. Upon completion of the egg-laying ritual, the female "doe" or "hen" steelhead stays in the area for several weeks. Unlike salmon, the steelhead does not die after the spawn. They return to the ocean, and about 10% will live to spawn a second time.

The fall migration steelhead try to jump Sherars Falls, where a fish ladder has been constructed to assist their travels up the river.

CHINOOK SALMON

The chinook salmon has had a powerful influence upon the cultural values of local Indian societies. It derives its name from the original Chinook Indian tribe located on the north bank at the mouth of the Columbia River. Other common names for this magnificent fish are king salmon, Columbia River salmon, tyee salmon, spring salmon, tule salmon, quinnat salmon, chowichee salmon and takou salmon.

The chinook is a robust, deep-bodied fish reaching lengths up to 5 feet and weights of 100 pounds. Commercially sold chinook demand the highest price of all salmon.

Ancestral Indians gathered at Celilo Falls for centuries in tribal fish-gathering rituals, at which they prepared their catch for year round food supplies. The fabulous wealth of the world's largest salmon run developed a cultural and social interchange between all of the Indian tribes in the Northwest. Celilo Falls became the hub of dozens of Indian trails which led from homelands to the great fishery.

Since the construction of the Dalles Dam, Celilo Falls no longer exists. Only the memories of proud Indian traditions are preserved in today's Chinook language and jargon. A whisper of the original fish catching method remains as descendants of the once great fishing society ceremoniously dip their giant nets into the Deschutes, searching for the legendary fish at Sherars Falls.

Hopefully, the Deschutes will become productive in the near future as plans for a large salmon fish hatchery are put into effect on the Warm Spring Reservation. The products derived from this hatchery may renew the once powerful bond between the Indian and the fish.

Major spawning migrations occur in the spring and a remnant run enters the river in the fall. Biologists report over 200 redds per mile in the upper reaches of the Deschutes. Pelton Dam has eliminated the run further upstream. Basically, the reproductive cycle is the same as the steelhead, with the exception that, after spawning, all chinook die.

Chinook Salmon.

INTRODUCTION TO VEGETATION

The most important factor which controls plant growth is the amount of rainfall. Whereas the annual precipitation on Mount Hood averages 130 inches per year, less than 10 inches per year falls in the Deschutes canyon. This arid condition results in a desert environment. Vegetation is reduced and trees are smaller.

Most rivers flow towards the ocean and the amount of moisture increases as they near the coast. The Deschutes river flows north and joins the Columbia, therefore it remains arid. Large, moisture loving trees such as Douglas Fir, hemlock and spruce cannot exist due to lack of moisture. The only conifers that can survive are semi-arid species such as Ponderosa Pine and Western Juniper. Broadleaf species are found only along the river's edge. Sage, small juniper and wild grasses are the only species which survive away from the water. By early summer they have become tinder-dry and present a constant danger to both man and animals. They can be almost spontaneously ignited and the resulting grass-fires may spread uphill at speeds greater than 50 miles per hour, destroying everything in their paths. The junipers' fire scarred trunks and gnarled lower limbs offer mute evidence of the effects of numerous grass-fires which have occurred in the canyon. However, the regular scorching of the earth has played an essential ecological role for centuries. It maintains the delicate balance between the grasses and the sage, providing sufficient food for grazing wildlife.

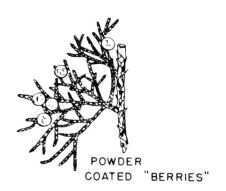

POWDER COATED "BERRIES"

Western Juniper.

a Juniper has no "typical" form? It assumes different forms, to "impersonate" other trees in their habitats. Half-dead, gnarled and ghostlike they tell of a constant, precarious struggle to survive where no other tree is able to live.

WHITE ALDER

Habit: Tree from 40 to 80 feet tall and 1 to 2 feet in diameter; grayish-brown scaly bark. *Leaves:* 2 to 3½ inches long; margins finely serrate to doubly serrate; green to yellowish-green; slightly sticky on upper surface; paler color on underside. *Fruit:* Winged nutlet borne in a semi-woody cone; ½ to ¾ inch long and brown in color. *Bark:* On older trunks, about 1 inch thick; whitish to grayish brown with flat, plated ridges which are superficially scaly. *Uses:* Popular nesting site for birds; provides important shade in the Deschutes canyon; not commercially important.

WESTERN JUNIPER

Habit: Medium-sized tree; may be more than 50 feet in height and more than 12 inches in diameter. *Leaves:* Tiny, scale-like; scratchy to the touch; each scale has a tiny gland or pit on the back where there is or was a minute, clear bead of resin. *Cones:* Bluish berry is considered to be a cone. *Bark:* Shreddy; thin; light to dark brown. *Uses:* Fence-posts, souvenirs and novelties; birds and small animals feed on the berries. *Comments:* Junipers are among the oldest trees in Oregon. Some species in the Whitehorse Rapids area exceed a thousand years of age. Juniper is known as the "camel" of our trees. It can live with less water than any other species of tree found in Oregon. Have you ever noticed that

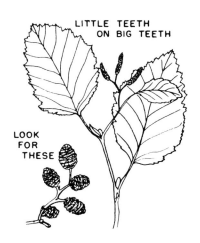

LITTLE TEETH ON BIG TEETH

LOOK FOR THESE

White Alder.

PONDEROSA PINE

Habit: Important large timber tree 125 to 180 feet tall, 3 to 6 feet in diameter. Yellow-brown bark in scaly plates. *Needles:* 3, sometimes 2, per bundle. *Cones:* 3 to 5 inches long (mostly 3 to 4 inches). Ovoid, green to purplish-brown prior to maturity, turning brown upon maturity. Armed with straight prickle. *Bark:* Young bark is brown to nearly black, ridged and furrowed. Turns yellowish-brown in furrows near base of tree, gradually spreading over ridges and up trunk. Scales of bark look like jigsaw puzzle parts. *Uses:* Millwork, boxes and crates, furniture, piling, poles, mine timbers and general construction. Probably the most important mill-work and general-use species in this part of the country.

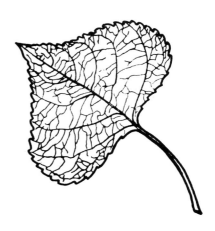

Poplar.

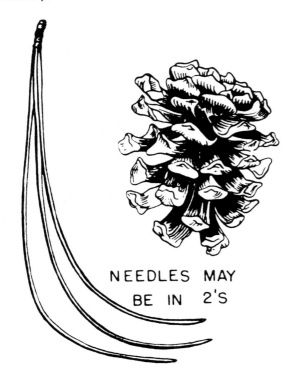

NEEDLES MAY BE IN 2'S

Ponderosa Pine.

POPLAR (Lombardi)

Habit: Tall, European tree with a columnar shape; 80 to 125 feet tall and 2 to 4 feet in diameter when fully grown. *Leaves:* 1¼ to 2½ inches long; almost triangular or diamond shaped; smooth and yellow-green above, paler green beneath. *Flowers:* None — they are all male trees. *Bark:* On younger trees it is comparatively smooth, later becoming grayish-black, deeply-ridged and furrowed on larger trees. *Comments:* Lombardi Poplars are indigenous to northern Italy. In the Deschutes canyon, this tree has been planted for windbreaks and erosion control. It sprouts vigorously from both the roots and the stump and may be steadily propogated from cuttings.

SAGEBRUSH

Habit: A small to large silvery-green shrub up to 15 feet tall, usually less. *Leaves:* Persistent, alternate, simple; silvery-green on both sides; ½ to 1½ inches long. *Flowers:* Small, yellowish, tubular; borne in long spikes. *Fruit:* Grayish-brown, splits lengthwise. *Uses:* Important browse for game animals and sheep. *Comments:* Sagebrush is the most abundant shrub in Central Oregon. The leaves emit a distinct strongly-scented odor when crushed.

Sagebrush.

SUMAC

Habit: Shrub up to 15 feet tall. *Leaves:* Deciduous; 8 to 14 inches long; pinnately compound with 9 to 24 leaflets; each leaflet is 1½ to 3 inches in length; dark green above, pale green or whitish green below. *Flowers:* Small, white, borne in dense clusters. *Fruit:* Bright red berry persistent year-round. *Bark:* Grayish brown. *Uses:* Browsed by deer; many game birds eat the fruit. *Remarks:* Foliage turns bright red in the fall.

BRIGHT CRIMSON FALL COLOR
BIG RED FRUIT CLUSTER

Sumac.

WILLOWS

Habit: Rapidly growing, thicket-forming trees and shrubs. *Leaves:* Deciduous, alternate, 5-ranked. Margins may be entire, wavy or serrate. *Flowers:* Forms catkins, sometimes fragrant. *Fruit:* Two-valved, 1-celled capsule, ¼ inch or less in length; contains several minute, hairy seeds. Seeds disseminate in late spring or early summer. Seed very short lived. Needs moist mineral soil. *Remarks:* Very intolerant. Occurs on many types of soil. Comparatively short lived, but prolific sprouters. Easily propogated by cuttings. Useful for erosion control.

PREPARATIONS FOR SAFETY AND HAZARDS

Proper footwear is essential when either in the boat or walking along the banks of the river. The correct choice of footwear will help eliminate slipping on rocks and boulders, which can cause serious injuries and spoil your trip. The best footing is obtained by wearing tennis shoes with either crepe or felt soles. You can "felt" your own shoes by cutting pieces out of indoor/outdoor carpeting and glueing the felt on the bottoms of your tennis shoes with an adhesive which is waterproof. Never let anyone in your party walk barefoot. It is always possible that a piece of glass, buried tin or other dangerous objects may be unexpectedly stepped on. The sharp, hard rocks can cut like a razor and the rounded boulders cause stubbed toes and unstable footing. During an emergency situation you cannot take the time to find and put on shoes which may have been removed because you did not anticipate problems.

Adequate cold-weather clothing must be taken. You can always take clothing off when you're too warm, but you can't put it on if you're cold if you haven't remembered to bring it with you. It is very helpful to dress in "layers" instead of wearing just one heavy jacket. Take at least one sweatshirt, one sweater and one light jacket. On whitewater trips you're likely to get drenched, so make sure your clothes are the quick-dry type. Rayon, nylon or other modern synthetic lightweight clothes dry much faster than cottons and woolens. However, for real warmth, there is no comparison between wet synthetics and wet woolens. Woolens will keep you warm under extreme conditions. Blue jeans are comfortable and tough, but they take hours to dry. Also, remember to carry lightweight raingear with you. It helps stop wind penetration and keeps you from becoming so cold and wet that your trip becomes unpleasant. A long-sleeved shirt or light jacket, and long-legged pants will control or prevent sunburn during your trip. A light color or reflective finish is best during sunny weather trips. Sunglasses and broad-brimmed hats control sun glare and excessive heat, preventing headaches, sunburned scalps, aching eyes and frayed tempers at the end of each day.

Waterproof bags should be included as part of your essential gear. They should contain your sleeping bags, clothing, delicate instruments and other sensitive gear which should remain dry and protected. Although plastic garbage bags are waterproof, they will not withstand the physical stress and abuse received during a typical river trip. Good waterproof bags may be purchased in military surplus stores and outdoor supply centers. The bags should be strong enough to serve as cushions, protective padding, emergency fabric and floating devices.

A waterproof ground cover or tarpaulin is also a very important piece of equipment. It can be used as a ground cloth to sleep on, a windbreak, a protective covering at camp to shelter food, firewood and people during rainstorms, a protective covering from morning dew on sleeping bags, a tablecloth for meals, a blanket and gathering place to discuss the day's experiences, a water-carrying device and an emergency fabric supply. In emergencies its material can be used to make ropes, emergency repairs, stretchers, hammocks, first-aid bandaging and slings.

A protective camera container can save you hundreds of dollars. An adequate container can range from a simple plastic bag to costly molded camera cases designed to be waterproof and shock resistant. It is important that whatever you choose be waterproof and airtight, so that your camera will be protected and float in case of capsizing. It is always a good idea to tie your camera container to the boat.

The Type 1 PFD (Personal Flotation Device)... This "lifejacket" is designed to keep your head out of water if you are knocked unconscious while in the river. If you are tossed out of your craft, sucked under or forced against rocks, you will feel a lot more secure with these heavy duty lifesaving jackets. They are also designed to prevent your body from slipping out of the jacket, which is a problem with the designs of some of the other life-jacket type flotation vests. Although Type 3 or Type 4 Personal Flotation Devices may look more stylish, they're simply not as safe. If traveling in a large group, bring an extra Type 1 lifejacket along. Kayakers should wear safety headgear, and be sure

of their abilities before entering the strong rapids of the Deschutes canyon.

A general repair kit should not just include materials for boat repairs, but should also contain miscellaneous other items to handle the repairs of all your other gear. Coleman lanterns should be accompanied by extra mantles, broken fishing rods and reels are an unpleasant (but common) occurrence, tent fabric tears appear unexpectedly. A thousand little problems may occur at some time during your years on the river. Be sure to include at least the following in your kit: some wire, cord, an assortment of nuts and bolts, glue, a needle and thread, pliers, gloves, an axe with a flat end to be used as a hammer or anvil, a selection of screwdrivers, a knife, patching material and resin/glue as required. Also include a candle for wax as a lubricant when you need it, vaseline, extra parts for specialized equipment which you take with you on your trip.

Try to anticipate hazards and inconveniences in advance, and outfit yourself with the necessary items which will help you work your way out of any unexpected difficulty. Have a pleasant trip!

Type 1 Lifejackets are safest.

SAMPLE GEAR LIST . . .

FLOATING DEVICE— Some will choose a drift boat, others a raft, kayak or inflatable boat. Whichever floating device you choose, remember to take adequate repairs for your vessel. A completely equipped boat should include the following items:

LIFE JACKET (TYPE 1)	BAIL BUCKET (plastic preferred)
AIR-PUMP (for inflatables)	EXTRA OARS or PADDLES
EXTRA OAR-LOCKS	EXTRA TIE-DOWN ROPES
LINING-ROPE (100 ft. length)	SPONGE (to cushion, wipe, bail)

PERSONAL GEAR— Each person will have his own preferences, of course, but the following items are recommended to make your trip comfortable and give you maximum versatility.

CHANGE OF PANTS/JEANS/SHORTS	LONG-SLEEVE SHIRT (avoid sunburn)
UNDERWEAR & SOCKS	BATHING SUIT
SWEATER or SWEATSHIRT	LIGHT JACKET
WALKING SHOES	HAT (broad-brimmed to avoid sunburn)
BOATING SHOES	TOWEL
FLASHLIGHT (with extra batteries)	SOAP
SUNGLASSES	SUN-TAN LOTION (or sunscreen lotion)
INSECT REPELLENT	CHAPSTICK (or other lip protector)
TOILET PAPER (or Kleenex tissue)	TOOTHBRUSH
SHAVING KIT (or electric razor)	TOOTHPASTE
POCKET KNIFE	KNIFE/FORK/SPOON/PLATE/CUP
WHISTLE (for safety, better than voice)	(carry these in web-sack for easy clean)
CANTEEN (for water)	GLOVES (protection from abrasion)
RAINGEAR (lightweight, waterproof)	DUFFEL BAG(S) (carry all efficiently)
6' x 8' POLYETHYLENE SHEET	

COOKING GEAR— You will probably need to eat during your river trip. Assuming you want to cook your food over an open fire or flame, you will need the following items as well as your food:

FRYING PAN (suitable for size of group)	GRATE (to place over coals)
DUTCH-OVEN (allows amazing versatility)	NESTING POTS/PANS (to suit needs)
CAN-OPENER (often forgotten)	SPATULA (mixing/scraping/turning)
LADLE(S) (for liquids)	LARGE SERVING/COOKING SPOONS
LONG-HANDLED FORKS	ALUMINUM FOIL
PAPER TOWELLING	SALT/PEPPER/SPICES/COOKING OIL
COFFEE POT	PLASTIC BUCKET (mix batter/salads)
PLASTIC JUICE CONTAINER	SCOURING PAD (a welcome aid)
LARGE METAL CONTAINER TO	SHARP KNIFE (cuts meat/lettuce/etc.)
HEAT DISHWATER (etcetera)	DISH TOWELS
TABLE CLOTH	LIQUID DISH SOAP/DETERGENT
GLOVES (protect hands from heat)	PLIERS (handle hot metal lids)
MATCHES (or reliable lighter)	FUEL (for stoves if fuel-stoves taken)

CAMPING GEAR— Some rugged individualists sleep with no protection or accessories. The rest of us will find the following items useful:

TENT	SHOVEL	ICE CHEST(S)
GROUNDSHEET	LANTERN	AXE (or saw)
FOAM PAD (or air-mattress)	SLEEPING BAG	PILLOW

FIRST-AID KIT— Accidents occur when you least expect them. They can be minor cuts, bruises or abrasions, or they can be major life-threatening crises. BE PREPARED — your kit should include the following, but anything additional may also be added:

ADHESIVE TAPE	GAUZE PADS	BAND-AIDS (all sizes)
ASPIRIN (or similar medicine)	TRIANGULAR BANDAGE	SPLINT(S)
SCISSORS	TWEEZERS (or forceps)	RAZOR-BLADE(S)
BLANKET(S)	SALT TABLETS	PETROLEUM JELLY
ABSORBENT COTTON	Q-TIPS (or similar product)	EYE-WASH & CUP
SUNBURN LOTION	ALCOHOL (or antiseptic)	SNAKE-BITE KIT

GLOSSARY

basalt: the dark, dense igneous rock of a lava flow.

black powder: old-fashioned blasting powder, replaced by modern day dynamite and plastic explosives.

brick bat basalt: the basalt which has cooled slowly, forming block-shaped structures resembling broken bricks jointed in two or more directions, rather than in columns like columnar basalt.

channel: when an island splits the river into two or more sections, the river forms two or more channels.

Clarno Formation: volcanic rock structure created in Eocene time.

Columbia River Basalt: one of the world's most extensive outpourings of lava which occurred some 15-35 million years ago.

compound leaf: a leaf composed of 2 or more leaflets.

deciduous plants: plants which lose their leaves each fall.

Deschutes Railroad: a railway constructed as a subsidiary of the Oregon-Washington Railroad and Navigation Company.

Eocene: a period of time beginning 60 million years ago and ending 40 million years ago.

John Day Formation: a volcanic rock formation created during the Oligocene period, from 35-50 million years ago.

lava: the molten rock that flows from a volcano.

lava tunnel: when the surface and sides of a volcanic lava flow cools before the core, and the core continues to flow, the central lava drains from the core, leaving an empty space, tube or tunnel.

line: to lower the boat through the rapids by the use of a lining rope.

midstream: the center of the river.

Oregon Trunk: a railway built as a subsidiary of the Spokane, Portland & Seattle Railway.

perlite: a volcanic glass. When a melt of any kind is cooled very rapidly, the atoms are frozen in the positions they occupied in the molten rock, forming natural glasses. Perlite is one type.

persistant leaves: remain on the tree all year.

pillow lava: when hot lava is extruded from the flow front underwater, the rapidly cooled lava forms pillow-shaped rocks. When you see pillow lava in sequence with bedrock, you can be sure they were formed under water.

Pleistocene: a period of time covered by the last million or so years, since the rise and dominance of man.

plug: a solid lava structure which was once inside a volcano. The cone of the volcano has since been eroded away by wind and water, leaving the hard, central core (or plug) standing like a giant finger pointing to the sky.

portage: to carry a boat around a rapids.

simple leaf: the leaf is composed of only one part.

talus: piles of small pieces of rock which have been broken away from a massive rock structure because of weathering. Talus structures are found at the bases of cliffs.